T0163283

Fly Heads and Bird Claws

蠅頭與鳥爪　梁秉鈞詩集

Published by MCCM Creations 2012
www.mccmcreations.com
info@mccmcreations.com

Poems 詩 / Leung Ping-kwan 梁秉鈞
Art 畫 / Lau Gukzik 劉掬色

Design / Lau Gukzik, Choy Yinga
設計 / 劉掬色，蔡怡雅

Contributors / Jonathan Chaves, Martha Cheung, Jennifer Feeley,
Brian Holton, Luo Hui, Helen Leung, Christopher Mattison, John
Minford, Glen Steinman, Afaa Michael Weaver and Michelle Yeh

Acknowledgements / eduArts, Dexter Lee
鳴謝 / 啟智藝術教育，李彥錚

ISBN 978-988-15217-8-1

蠅頭與鳥爪

Fly Heads and Bird Claws

梁秉鈞詩集

Leung Ping-kwan

mccmcreations

Contents
目錄

III

IV

V

Rice is our common language
Rice is our consoling mother
Rice encompasses all colours
Rice soothes a stomach's wounds

—Leung Ping-kwan from "Nasi Kuning"

It is fitting that a majority of conversations with Leung Ping-kwan occur around dishes of food: at a Harvard Square restaurant during his Fulbright year in 2006, over snacks at a Mid-Autumn Festival reading at Chinese University, in a CityU restaurant discussing the state of translation, and compiling lists of Hong Kong authors while overlooking Kowloon from a vegetarian café.

Food is not so much a recurrent theme in Leung's writing as it is a metaphysical imperative. One must eat, just as one must cogitate the reason for eating and then write. As Rey Chow notes in her introduction to Leung's 2002 poetry collection *Travelling with a Bitter Melon*, "a closer look at Leung's other work reveals he has, in fact, been consistently drawing on what can be eaten for his imaginative, multi-generic cartographies . . ."[1] His palate becomes a road map for quotidian and universal concerns.

When asked to respond to Chow's statement at a restaurant in Causeway Bay, and to provide a frame for his recent writing, Leung did not answer immediately. He chose first a slice of tofu, some deep fried eggplant, ginger, and then responded:

Yong wu shi.
Poetry about things.

Preface   Christopher Mattison

Taking this statement at its most transparent level, these "things" are most often: food, Hong Kong culture, East/West hybrids, which is largely how this present volume has been divided. However, it is the first of this trifecta that resonates across each of the themes. Foods are set forth to act both as flavors unto themselves and as links to past and future realms, as in the poem "Boiled Beancurd":

> no gold or silver or desire, just beancurd
> not even dried mushrooms, beansprouts
> we have come directly to an extraordinary place of Zen
> not breathing the smoke of the world, just eating beancurd

It obviously "just is" and is "not just" beancurd. One *must* eat, but one also is necessarily led by the associations with larger constructs. Narratives of colonialism, cultural identity, exile and displacement all find a voice through the various tastes, as in this stanza on Vietnamese stuffed snails:

> I was plucked out
> Removed from
> My geography and history
> Given exotic colors
> Foreign flavors
> Added value
> Higher price
> All to place me
> Into some future
> Unknown
>
> *(Hap La Gung, 2002)*

[1] Leung Ping-kwan, *Travelling with a Bitter Melon*, Edited by Martha P. Y. Cheung with Foreword by Rey Chow, (Hong Kong: Asia 2000 Limited, 2002), p. 9.

Or in "Fragrant Guava" (2008), which details Leung spending an entire day wandering Taipei in search of one particular type of guava, having been disappointed by what he'd found in the first market and a friend's earlier promise of a mythic sweetness. Food is a synesthetic trigger that links Leung to various locales and eras, so that even when he is toying with traditional formats and writing of some other "thing", the gustatory sidles in.

Six years after eating with Leung in Harvard Square, he still remembers, without prompting, the particular spice used in the samosas; the weight on the fork. He is the consummate tour guide, able to direct readers from kitchen tables through urban and interior landscapes that are mottled with Cantonese, Mandarin, numerous Englishes, and a cascade of other cultures. This ability to create in a hybrid space without sounding forced or inauthentic has evolved throughout his writing career that began in the late 1960s, through PhD work in comparative literature at the University of California, San Diego in the 1980s, and then back to Hong Kong for a long career of intertwining writing and teaching at several universities. Leung has been influential not just as a writer, but also as an educator and administrator dedicated to expanding the humanities across Hong Kong.

Beyond his own writing and teaching, it is worth highlighting that over the decades Leung has been a major inspiration for and a tireless proponent of his fellow Hong Kong writers. Before relocating to Hong Kong in 2010, I had been working on a literature survey detailing the availability of Hong Kong writing in English translation, both as a primer for myself and as a way of helping to come to terms with various definitions of world literature. The survey did not get very far. The university library contained two anthologies and half a dozen single-author collections, primarily in the Renditions series. As for the web-based survey, two particularly non-encyclopedic entries listed a total of six "renowned" Hong Kong poets—Leung Ping-kwan, Ye Si, PK Leung, Liang Bingjun, Ping Kwan, and Bei Dao.

Bei Dao has been resident in Hong Kong for the last several years as a new generation of southbound writer, but anyone familiar with his work understands that his thematic concerns and poetics remain rooted elsewhere. The other six poets mentioned are all, of course, the author of this collection—Leung Ping-kwan, who has also written for decades under the pen name Ye Si.

So, what is the basis for Leung's recognition, in relation to the near silence that surrounds other Hong Kong writers?—save for a few works by Xi Xi and Eileen Chang in English translation. Leung certainly has benefited from the support of a range of international scholars and translators—Martha Cheung, Brian Holton, Rey Chow, David Der-wei Wang, Afaa Weaver, Lee Ou-Fan Lee and John Minford, to name but a few. It certainly has made a difference that Leung has consistently written across the genres, from narrative poetry to post-modern criticism, film surveys to experimental novels, cultural studies of Hong Kong to food criticism. It is also significant that he has spent time studying and lecturing in the U.S. and Europe, and works comfortably in a range of modes, from western-centric theories to more local, and decolonial assessments of home.

Leung's most recent awards have included an Honorary Doctoral Degree in Literature (presented by the University of Zürich, Switzerland) and the Writer of the Year Award, presented at the 2012 Hong Kong Book Fair. In 2011, Leung received the Hong Kong Bi-annual Literary Award (organized by the Hong Kong Public Library) for the best work of fiction in Chinese, 2009-2011 (*Post-colonial Affairs of Food and the Heart*), and in that same year he also received a Hong Kong Arts Development Award. With recognition comes the power for advocacy, and as Leung notes in his study of Hong Kong colonialism, "Hong Kong literature has yet to sort out its history and to compile its anthologies."[2] But the work is being done, and in no small part to Leung Ping-kwan. In terms of the remaining Hong Kong literary landscape, as already noted, Leung has exerted a significant amount of energy on attempting to increase the visibility of all Hong Kong writing; most recently as one of the driving forces behind Lingnan University's publication *A Bibliography of Hong Kong Literature in Foreign Languages*.

This bibliography features a cumulative sweep of foreign translations of Hong Kong literary works into 15 languages, including English, French, Japanese and Korean, along with work translated into Arabic, Greek, Yugoslavian, and other languages of "lesser diffusion". The publication of this bibliography is a significant next step in identifying the key authors and available works, so that editors, translators, and publishing houses can familiarize themselves with the writing and make educated decisions moving forward. Leung is fascinated by modes of representation, by the permanent flux that is Hong Kong, and by the challenges involved in conveying to permanent flux that is Hong Kong, and by the challenges involved in conveying to readers a spectrum of lives. Or as Martha Cheung effectively distills Leung's creative output—his work expands "from poetic discovery to political intervention":

The city is always the colour of neon
Secret messages hidden there
The pity is only, you're wearing a mask
No way to know if it's you that's speaking

Fruit from many different places
Each with its own tale to tell
In newly dressed shop windows
Che Guevara rhymes with the latest in shoes

(Cityscape, 2003)

These elements are "a shared chance discovery, some carefully drawn interior montage, where intimacy is slowly and delicately etched".[3] Discussion of Hong Kong's neon and myriad shop windows in "Cityscape" reintroduces the "things" and their function, while instigating a socio-political critique of what has become the new window, for the Mainland, onto the West. Which simultaneously leads to a discussion of metaphor and Chinese versus pan-Western traditions. How do the objects relate to the unsaid layers of language and historical constructs? What do they signify? Is there a code? Are they "just" things? Again, they are and are not, as explained by Leung during a recent interview:

---

[2] Leung Ping-kwan, "Two Discourses on Colonialism: Huang Guliu and Eileen Chang on Hong Kong of the Forties", in *Modern Chinese Literary and Cultural Studies in the Age of Theory: Reimagining a Field*, Edited by Rey Chow, (Durham and London: Duke University Press, 2000), p. 79.

[3] Leung Ping-kwan, *Islands and Continents: Short Stories by Leung Ping-kwan*, Edited by John Minford with Brian Holton and Agnes Hung-chong Chan, (Hong Kong: Hong Kong University Press, 2007), p. ix.

I feel that the genre of writing about "things" exhausted itself by the time of the Qing dynasty, due in large part to the narrow practice of merely using the form as a moral lesson (the "thing" as a vehicle to carry a message) or as a word puzzle to be deciphered (where the language within the poem is there simply for the reader to guess at the object being described).

In my work I want to 1) write a kind of modern poetry that does not have to turn away from the world we live in, does not have to recede into language in a solipsistic way, but rethinks the relationship between language and objects. 2) I also would like to readjust to read the world from the perspective of simple objects, rather than from the viewpoint of monuments or hero status. 3) I want my poems about things to be a dialogue with the world; not to project upon them a moral statement, but to learn and be inspired by their shapes, smells and colours, and to develop a new vocabulary with which to write. (Leung interview, 2012)[4]

This new vocabulary is based in humility and a curiosity in melding traditional modes with present-day concerns. Not in the sense of the modern classical poems that continue to fill Mainland journals, but in using the concision found at the core of traditional forms (both Western and Chinese) to give shape to the constantly evolving geopolitical space of "The Asia Century".

China is a *cheongsam* on a calendar
We could easily become decals on a bicycle
A lover's eye on a matchbox
Haute couture and cigarette butts form clubs
Blood and sweat or spilled soy sauce,
neither blood nor fervor is convincing now
Onions and garlic meet again after a long exile
Speaking in whispers on into the night

(Mao Salad at the Paris China Club, 2000)

Fly Heads and Bird Claws is the most recent in a long line of Leung projects that converge translators and the visual arts. Gukzik's vibrant illustrations and Leung's poetry entwine to impress taste via color in a shifting map of Hong Kong dishes and foreign tables. Simple ink drawings follow thumbprints of color, secret family recipes, ruins, sticky rice, a lone pepper. In "Mao Salad", Leung's eye fuses commodified objects into a love song for his city. The reader falls into a wash of color while considering the transition of Hong Kong's bygone markets to the present-day reality of "vintage" market places. This particular eye has developed, in part, thanks to the numerous ekphrastic projects that have kept Leung in conversation with fellow writers, visual artists, fashion designers, and translators. This is the work of an exacting creative artist who will continue to watch and detail the city for years to come; one tongue upon the world of Leung's past, and a future Hong Kong that awaits to be imagined and read.

[4] Interview with Leung Ping-kwan, with Christopher Mattison, Causeway Bay, Hong Kong, April 2012.

米飯是我們共通的語言
米飯是我們安慰的母親
米飯包容不同的顏色
米飯燙貼腸胃裏舊日的傷痕
—— 梁秉鈞,〈印尼黃飯〉

大多數我與梁秉鈞的對話均恰切地圍繞餐桌進行:不論是2006年他作為傅爾布萊特學者時我們在哈佛廣場的一間餐廳裏傾談,或是在中文大學某個中秋節讀詩會淺嚐小點,還是於城市大學餐廳討論翻譯進度,又或是在一間素食館邊整理香港作家名單,邊眺望九龍半島。

食物不單是梁秉鈞作品中反覆出現的主題,它更多時候是一種形而上的追求。人必須吃,正如人必須深思吃的原因,然後才寫作。周蕾為梁秉鈞2002年的詩選《帶一枚苦瓜旅行》寫序,「細看梁氏其他創作,你會發現他多年來其實一直藉食物繪製出他心目中充滿想像力、跨類別的圖譜⋯⋯」[1],他以味覺串聯起日常瑣碎的、平凡的東西。

在銅鑼灣一所素食館,我問起他對周氏的看法,並要他概括一下自己最近的創作。他不慌不忙,先夾起一片豆腐,茄子和薑芽,然後回答:

詠物詩
與東西有關的詩

這句子中的「東西」，簡單來說，指的往往是：食物、香港本土文化、東/西混雜，這同時亦是本書最主要的劃分。然而，食物是此三重奏中貫穿書中每個主題之首。食物既代表它們各自的味道，也連繫着過去與未來，就如〈湯豆腐〉中的詩句：

> 沒有金銀和慾望，只有豆腐
>
> 連冬菇也沒有，連豆芽也沒有
>
> 我們簡直已經到了非常禪的境界
>
> 不吃人間煙火，只是吃豆腐

顯然，它就是、但也不單單只是豆腐。人必須吃，但人同樣有必要與大概念連繫。殖民主義、文化認同、流徙與離散的論述都能透過各種口味找到一把聲音，就如越南〈釀田螺〉中的一節：

> 把我拿出來
>
> 使我遠離了
>
> 我的地理和歷史
>
> 加上異鄉的顏色
>
> 加上外來的滋味
>
> 給我增值
>
> 付出了昂貴的代價
>
> 為了把我放到
>
> 我不知道的
>
> 將來

[1] 梁秉鈞著、張佩瑤編：《帶一枚苦瓜旅行》，香港：Asia 2000，2000，第9頁。

又如〈軟香的芭樂〉，它談到梁氏不滿意在一般菜市找到的芭樂(番石榴)，嚐不到朋友向他保證的那種獨特的芬芳，在台北遊蕩一整天，尋找一種特別品種的芭樂。食物是使到梁氏與不同的語言環境和時代連繫起來的觸媒。因此，即使他把玩着傳統格律和寫着別些「東西」的時候，這種味覺竟又悄然浮現。

哈佛廣場一會的六年之後，梁秉鈞仍然沒有忘記咖喱角用的特別香料，和食物的份量。他是一位精湛的導遊，能夠帶引讀者從廚房的餐桌，穿越廣東文化、各種漢語或英語文化、以及其他不同文化交錯的大城小景。他這種創造混雜空間的能力，真實而無絲毫勉強或造作之感，早在60年代開始寫作生涯時逐漸發展成形，至 80 年代於聖地牙哥加州大學修讀比較文學博士、及後返回香港邊寫作邊在大學任教，一直穩定發展。梁氏一直以來的影響力不只在於他是一名作家，也關乎他是教育工作者和致力在香港推廣人文關注的執行人。

寫作和教學之外，他一直是香港後輩作家的一個主要啟蒙者。2010年我移居香港之前，一直在從事一個詳述香港文學英譯可行性的研究，這既為我日後的工作打下基礎，也幫助香港文學打入世界文學之列。這項研究並沒能走得很遠——原因是大學圖書館裏只有兩冊香港文學選集和六本個別作者的作品結集，主要出現在譯叢系列；而網上兩個非百科全書的條目中列出共有六位「著名」的香港詩人，他們分別是Leung Ping-kwan (梁秉鈞)、Ye Si (也斯)、PK Leung (梁 秉鈞)、Liang Bingjun (梁秉鈞)、Ping Kwan (秉鈞)，以及 Bei Dao (北島)。

北島在過去的幾年居於香港，是新一代的南來作家，但熟悉他著作的人都會知道，他關注的主題和他的詩作仍然植根別處。而其他六位上面提到的詩人，全是這本詩選的作者梁秉鈞，過去數十年他一直以筆名也斯創作小說散文。

除了西西和張愛玲有英文翻譯作品以外，相對其他無聞的香港作家，梁秉鈞為甚麼那麼受外國人認識？梁氏當然得益於一批國際學者和翻譯者的支持，包括張佩瑤、Brian Holton、周蕾、王德威、蔚雅風、李歐梵及約翰‧閔福德等等，不能一一盡錄。梁一貫書寫跨類別的作品，從敘事詩到後現代評論，電影研究到實驗小說，香港文化研究到食評，多變的風格令他顯得獨特。而且，他曾在美國和歐洲研究和講學，從以西方為中心的理論，到較本土的論述，及以解殖民地的角度審視故土，各種模式下他都能揮灑自如。

梁氏最近獲得的榮譽，包括由瑞士蘇黎世大學頒發的文學榮譽博士學位，以及 2012 年香港書展選為香港年度作家。2011年，梁氏藉《後殖民食物與愛情》一書，在香港公共圖書館舉辦的2009至2011香港文學雙年獎中，獲得最佳中文小說獎。同年，他還獲得香港藝術發展獎。聲名帶來倡議的力量，梁氏在他的香港殖民主義研究中提到「香港文學仍需理清歷史與編纂文選」。[2]現在這工作已在進行，當中不少是梁氏一手催成的。正如前段指出，梁秉鈞已努力不懈，試圖增加整個香港文學的知名度。最近，他便促成嶺南大學出版《香港文學外譯書目》。

此書目特別介紹過往的香港文學外譯作品，涵蓋十五種外語，包括英文、法文、日文、韓文，也有介紹翻譯成阿拉伯文、希臘文、南斯拉夫文，以及其他少眾語言的作品。這書目的出版在肯定主要作家及他們的作品方面無疑是向前跨了一大步，有助編輯、翻譯者及出版社熟讀這些創作，有系統地推廣香港作品。梁氏着迷於不同模式的表達方式，香港持續不斷的變遷，和向讀者傳達多樣生活方式的挑戰。也許我們可以借張佩瑤對他創作精闢論述，看他如何「從詩情畫意中看見政治」：

> 城市總有霓虹的燈色
>
> 那裏有隱密的訊息
>
> 只可惜你戴起了口罩
>
> 聽不清楚是不是你在說話
>
> 來自不同地方的水果
>
> 各有各敘說自己的故事
>
> 櫥窗有最新的構圖
>
> 革命孩子和新款鞋子押韻
>
> 〈城市風景，2003〉

這些元素均是「一個共享的偶遇，一些精心繪製的內心蒙太奇，緩慢而微妙地滲溢着親切的氣息」。[3]〈城市風景〉中對香港霓虹燈和無數商店櫥窗的討論，重新審視「事物」和它們的功能，也對香港成為中國眺望西方的窗子，提出了一個新的社會政治性的批判。這同時引起了一個有關隱喻和中/西方傳統的討論：物件如何跟未明言的語言和歷史結構扯上關係？它們意味着甚麼？有沒有規則？他們是否就「只是」東西？答案是雙重的，梁氏在最近一次訪問中解釋到：

> 我感覺到了清末，詠物詩的文類已逐漸式微了，大多因為創作
> 者都只是狹隘地借詠物說教(以之作為盛載訊息的工具)，或以
> 為詠物就是提出一個有待破解的文字謎語（詩中的語言純粹供
> 讀者猜測描述對象之用）。

> 在我的作品中，我有三個想法。第一，我想寫一種無需遠離我
> 們生活的世界、無需退回艱深堂皇語言建構世界，而是反思語
> 言和對象之間的關係。第二，我想由簡單而非宏大的日常事物
> 去看世界，重新調整閱讀世界的角度。第三，我希望這些詠物
> 詩是與世界對話的詩，不在物件身上強加道德教義，而是去欣
> 賞它們的形狀、氣味和顏色，受它們啟發，並發展出一組新的
> 書寫詞彙。〈摘錄自2012年訪問〉[4]

謙卑和糅合傳統模式與現世關注的好奇心是這組新詞彙的基礎。它並非充斥
內地期刊的那些現代古典詩詞，而是挪用在傳統形式（不論中西）的精髓中
找到的一種簡潔，以之塑造「亞洲世紀」不斷變化的地緣政治空間。

> 中國不過是月份牌上的旗袍
> 你我輕易變成自行車的擺設
> 火柴盒上有愛人的瞳孔
> 所有的虛榮和華服
> 與煙盅盅的煙蒂組織俱樂部

[2] 梁秉鈞著、周蕾編，〈殖民主義的兩個論述：黃谷柳與張愛玲筆下的
四十年代香港〉，《理論時代下的現代中國文學和文化研究：學科的
重新想像》，杜倫、倫敦：杜肯大學出版社，2000，第79頁。

[3] 梁秉鈞著、約翰、閔福德、Brian Holton、陳虹莊編，《島和大陸——
梁秉鈞短篇故事》，香港：香港大學出版社，2007，第ix頁。

[4] 梁秉鈞訪問，Christopher Mattison，香港，2012年四月。

流血流淚或是傾倒醬油

激情與熱血已不令人信服

蔥蒜經歷流亡與豉椒重逢

耳邊盡是有說不盡的話

〈巴黎「中國俱樂部」吃毛沙拉，2000〉

《蠅頭與鳥爪》是梁秉鈞一系列結合翻譯和視覺藝術的長遠創作中的最新作品。書中本土藝術家劉掬色的生動畫作和梁氏的詩歌交錯互動，為香港本土菜色和異鄉餐桌變化的地圖交替着色入味。家藏食譜祕方、廢墟斷垣，菜肉糯米飯、一枚辣椒，均可以簡單利落的線條和色調入畫。〈巴黎「中國俱樂部」吃毛沙拉〉中，梁的眼睛在各種商品中看見城市的情歌；讀者就在思考香港從昔日市集過渡到現代增值的古風市場時，沉浸於輪轉的斑斕色彩中。這種特殊的視野早經發展，部分因為梁氏一直讓詩與其他藝術接觸，與資深作家、視覺藝術家、時裝設計師，以及翻譯者保持對話。作者梁秉鈞是一位嚴謹且具創造力的藝術家，他將於往後的年月裏繼續觀察、敘述我們的城市。細讀詩篇，我們將能細味梁氏過往身處的世界，同時慢慢咀嚼一個有待想像和閱讀的、屬於未來的香港。

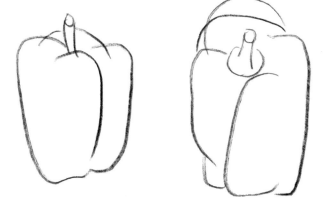

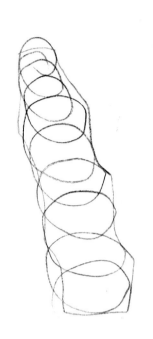
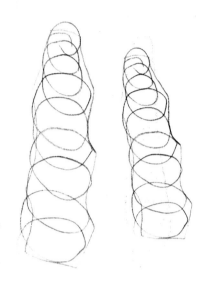

Picking Plums
Variations on Hong Kong Nursery Rhymes

our little Jenny
stole a little penny
to buy a bun
muck instead of make-up
crack-pot on her head
just for fun

run run run
run down the road
and pick a plum
sweet sweet plum
good road to run

ginger and coconut sandwich
a dozen kinds of scrambled egg
granny next door—baking a bun
"smell good, son?"
say no, get a smack—on the bum

run run run
run down the road
and get a rhyme
funny funny rhyme
good road to run

little master Jackie
bought some sugarcane, gone all yucky
bought some biscuits, gone all holey
always at the midden getting brooms
in the midden getting strange strange dreams

2004
Translated by Brian Holton

執個橙

阿蘇蘇
偷錢買鬆糕
有粉唔搽搽鑊撈
有帽唔戴
戴個爛沙煲

行行行 行行行
行到街邊執個橙
橙好鮮甜路好行

椰子夾酸薑
雞蛋撈埋十五樣
隔離婆仔燒炮仗
問你響唔響
唔響打阿蘇兩巴掌

行行行 行行行
行到街邊執句話
話好盞鬼路好行

阿蘇公 唔知搵乜東東
買碌蔗 又生虫
買個餅 又穿窿
成日係垃圾堆執竹筒
垃圾堆裏執出奇怪夢

2004
* 改編自香港童謠

The Human-faced Olive*

bitter green skin gripping the self tight
and always attracting incoherent encounters
unwilling to be mistaken for olive or cloudberry
always wanting to tell its own flavour

hugs and knocks leave black stripes behind
on the plate they suffer gentle steaming
no longer bothered by slowly-stretching skin
exposing the world-weary face on the kernel

softer and gentler, but they're summer's sourness still
infecting a thousand dishes and being infected again
reviving these many years numbed appetites
still looking for a fresh start beyond the banquet

1999
Translated by Brian Holton

* Also known as Chinese *dragonplum*

人面

青澀的表皮緊抓住自我
又總招引不相干的邂逅
不願被誤當橄欖或山稔
老想說清楚自已的味道

擁抱過也碰傷留下黑斑
在盤中飽經文火的蒸熬
不再計較皮膚緩緩舒開
露出了核上滄桑的人面

柔和了又仍是夏日酸澀
感染千重菜餚又被感染
翻新多年來已麻木胃口
飽饜外再尋清新的開始

1999

Boiled Beancurd

first on the white tablecloth
is set a bowl of beancurd
we begin to talk
imagining how from two-dimensions we'll cut reality away
into four square fields, all different
imagining we're simple farmers
imagining we're monks in meditation
the monastic evening meal only clear broth and beancurd
no mobile phones
no shares, no property speculation
no gold or silver or desire, just beancurd
not even dried mushrooms, not even beansprouts
we have come directly to the extraordinary place of Zen
not breathing the smoke of this world, just eating beancurd
but eating beancurd and chatting
we realise too that beancurd has many forms
like koya tofu for instance
in Japanese jails, prison visitors bring koya tofu so
you can squeeze out a half bottle of sake on the sly!
I say that I have eaten the light green crab roe beancurd
you say beancurd with shrimps and pine nuts
in the Edo period there was even a monograph: *100 Beancurd Treasures*
we've all eaten ham and beancurd
prawn and yamane tofu
Pocky Ma's Beancurd
stinky beancurd
we've touched on every flavour
and then there's mudfish beancurd
mudfish pushed into boiling water, with no escape
then made to squirm into ice-cold beancurd
to gratify our lust for good food
oh, Amida Buddha!
the more we talk, the worse we get
didn't we say we wanted concentration and discipline
and just have plain boiled beancurd?

湯豆腐

開始時在白布的桌面上
端來一碗湯豆腐
我們開始說話
從平面開始想像，把現實割切
阡陌縱橫許多不同的四方田
想像我們是樸實的農夫
想像我們是入定的老僧
寺門內晚膳只有清湯與豆腐
沒有手提電話
沒有股票與炒樓
沒有金銀和慾望，只有豆腐
連冬菇也沒有，連豆芽也沒有
我們簡直已經到了非常禪的境界
不吃人間煙火，只是吃豆腐
可是吃着豆腐，閒聊着
又想到了豆腐也有各種做法
比方說高野豆腐
坐牢時探監的人送來高野豆腐
可以偷偷榨出半壺清酒呢！
我說我有我以前吃過的
淺綠色的蟹膏豆腐
你說蝦仁松子豆腐
江戶時代就有豆腐百珍的專書

我們都吃過火腿豆腐
蝦子山根豆腐
麻婆豆腐
臭豆腐
各種味道都說起來了
還有泥魚的豆腐呢
驅使燙熱無處可走的泥魚
教牠們鑽進冰涼的冷豆腐裏
滿足我們美味的慾望
唉，阿彌陀佛
愈說愈不像樣了
我們不是說要收心養性
只吃一味湯豆腐的嗎？

2004

Yellow Pepper

Yellow pepper
Red pepper
I love your shine
Lighting up my kitchen table
From the breakfast bowl
Beginning with no explanation
Rushing to a messy end
Newly-derailed flavours
Leave behind such joy

You are a lovely tapestry
You are a small town in the rain
I'm grateful you came so far
Came into my menu to play
In a thick, rich fish soup
Emitting your aroma
Eaten with an ordinary cheese
Adding leaping colours
You are my daily fare

You are a city with hot springs
A hometown excelling in embroidery
You are a big single-span bridge
Music's shattered completeness
You borrow the violin's shoulder
To steal a long view from the castle's round window
Could be comic but never mediocre
You are last night's warm bed
Just able to contain new imaginings

Growing up with the sea winds blowing
Your heart may have been warmed
Body a proud lantern
You are a dancing puppet
A farmer singing opera
You're a real character
But you're never pungent
You are a child in poverty
But you're never shabby

In a pot of thick, rich beef stew
Each gladdening slice refreshes
You are a naughty soprano
From the tangle of plant connections
Showing your own crisp smile
Yellow pepper
Red pepper
I will always stand by you
A flavour that defies mediocrity

1998
Translated by Brian Holton

黃色的辣椒

黃色的辣椒
紅色的辣椒
我愛你的明亮
照亮了我的餐檯
從早餐的碟子上
不由分說地開始
匆忙混亂地結束
剛剛出軌的味道
留下愉快的感覺

你是艷麗的掛氈
你是微雨的小城
感謝你遠道而來
進入我的菜單遊戲
在濃濃的魚湯裏
散發自己的味道
與平凡的乳酪同吃
增加跳脫的顏色
你是我每日的營養

你是有溫泉的城市
你是擅長刺繡的故鄉
你是沒有橋墩的大橋
音樂裏破碎的完整
你借來小提琴的肩膀
古堡裏偷望遠方的圓窗
可能滑稽但卻絕不平庸
你是昨夜的溫床
剛好容得下新的想像

在海風吹刮之下長大
你的心可以變得溫軟
身體是驕傲的燈籠
你是跳舞的木偶
唱歌劇的農民
你有鮮明的個性
但你並不辛辣
你是貧窮的孩子
但你並不寒酸

一窩濃濃的牛肉雜燴裏
叫人開顏的片片清爽
你是頑皮的高音
從糾纏不清的植物關係裏
展開自己以爽脆的笑容
黃色的辣椒
紅色的辣椒
我會永遠支持你
對抗平庸的口味

1998

Dried Pak Choi

It will only be tasty after a year has gone by?
It will only turn golden as our days pass us by?

I never knew what it was
that Granny stored away
those rustling, many-layered
and many-leafed secrets

I loved the fresh green of youth
I loved the skin's bloom
that vanishes with a touch
a fresh life or a dried one
leading to a life unknown

I never liked the wrinkles on granny's face
never liked granny's black clothes
she was always bringing stuff out
was that our gathered-up and pleated past?

was there really once a healthy body inside the black and blue one?
Granny, let me try your soup to see if the gold of our days was in it

2004
Translated by Brian Holton

菜乾

要隔了一個年頭才好味道？
日子久了才會變得金黃？

過去我一直不知道
阿婆收藏起的是甚麼東西
那些窸窸窣窣的
層層多葉的祕密

總喜歡青翠的年華
喜歡吹彈得破的肌膚
一個潮濕的生命一個繃緊的生命
來到一個不知怎麼樣的生命

我從前不喜歡阿婆的滿臉縐紋
不喜歡阿婆的黑色衣衫
老是從裏面摸出一些甚麼來
那就是我們打了褶的過去嗎？

你說瘀青的身體裏真的曾有矯健的身體？
阿婆讓我再嚐你煮的湯看裏面有沒有日子的金黃

2004

Chaozhou Sauces

My dear,
I also think it's wonderful
how a green olive can be marinated into black
and vegetables diffuse their
flavors in a bowl of white porridge
giving it the flavor of a multifaceted world

Small white fish, tiny Nange and the Vegetarian fish—
so, which sauce?
Butterfly shrimp and crab—
plum sauce?
Puning tofu—
dip in saline water and coriander?
Goose innards and goose slices
waiting to be toned down in white vinegar

Are you freshly picked mustard greens
hoping to be marinated into sour or salted greens in my embrace?
You become the soft and sour
I'm the southern ginger powder on top
Pipa shrimp is a sweet maiden,
what taste shall I offer to match your simplicity?
You spend an entire morning brewing the strongest Kungfu tea
that'll keep you awake all night
I have to dim my glamour
absorb your strong flavor with my plain essence

What goes with sweet plum sauce?
What goes with pepper and vinegar?
What goes with Puning bean paste?
What goes with sugar and balsamic vinegar?
Each has a life and love of it's own
paired by chance
and what else is there to say

2004   Translated by the Author

潮州蘸醬

親愛的
我也覺得那是奇妙的
青色的欖如何醃成黑色
菜如何醃出各種味道
滲向一碗白粥
帶給它大千世界的滋味

白飯魚、南哥仔和齋魚
蘸怎樣的醬油？
蝴蝶蝦和螃蟹
需要梅醬嗎？
普寧豆腐
蘸鹽水和芫荽？
鵝腸鵝片和墨魚
等白醋來調和

你是新採的芥菜嗎？
想在我懷裏醃成酸菜還是鹹菜？
你變成了酸酸的大芥菜頭
我是你上面的南薑粉
琵琶蝦是蝦姑娘
我用什麼味道來配合你的樸素
花你一個早晨沏好的工夫茶
喝下去一個晚上不能成眠
我要把自己去盡繁華
以平淡的肉身接受你的濃烈

甚麼蘸甜的梅醬？
甚麼蘸辣椒和醋？
甚麼蘸普寧豆醬？
甚麼蘸糖和黑醋？
各有前因各有各的姻緣
剛好配上
就沒甚麼話好說了

2004

Comprador Soup

Taking pride in your creamy face?
Underneath the smooth surface
one wonders what lurks in secrecy
To whom is the shark's fin offered?
Dragging out old time legends of the ancestors
delicacies easily taken as common stuff

Between the differences in prices
how's sweet profit gained?
Yesterday the leftover of salty-fish stalls
today the delicacies waiting for the highest bid
You match-make affection on the palm of a hand
Anyone can propose to shrimps or sea bass at will

Who's not haggling around us?
No one puts a scale in the air
A retractable measuring tape in the pocket
abacus beads going up and down
Those from four corners of the land seeking their own place
praying for customers to flood in and goods to fly off shelves

Was there a child in you and me on the merry-go-round?
dizzy from drinking too much or spinning too fast?
Gamble all you have to take on a roller-coaster ride
All fall down
The thick paste of wealth seemingly bottomless
is but petty profit watered down?

2004
Translated by Brian Holton

金必多湯

以奶油的臉孔驕人？
滑溜的表面底下
不知有甚麼乾坤
把魚翅向誰獻寶？
搬出老祖宗陳年的傳說
山珍海錯容易當了平常

如何在價格的差異間
賺取美味的利潤？
昨天是鹹魚欄裏的剩貨
今天是待價而沽的珍饈
把感情的買賣玩弄於股掌
誰都可隨意投入小蝦或是石斑

咫尺間人人不都在討價還價？
沒有誰在天空上放一把天平
至少口袋裏的軟尺伸縮自如
算盤的各子不住上上下下
來自五湖四海分別找到自己的位置
蒙誰眷顧客似雲來貨如輪轉

旋轉木馬上可有你我的童心？
暈眩因為喝醉還是轉得太快
賭這一回所有財物如過山快車
突然墜落谷底
盡似無底深淵的富貴濃稠
可是蠅頭小利粉末和了開水？

2004

Fragrant Guava

Tempted by the light greens under the market lamps
last night I bought fresh guavas in the market
Large heads of green promise, so fresh
yet rough and dry when you bite down
Why this tasteless flesh?
I don't want to savor the shallow seeds of the times

Thanks for being with me today, wandering through alleys
Will there be other varieties on the other side of the city?
Did I smell the fragrance before or simply imagine it?
Where tender skin is nurtured by a loving embrace
sweet and mature, melting in the mouth
No sign of it yet? Thanks for searching with me.

2008
Translated by the Author

軟香的芭樂

被市場燈下的淺綠誘惑
昨天買回剛上市的芭樂
大顆青青答允無限清新
咬下去，滿口盡是乾澀
怎麼是這麼沒有味道的東西？
我拒絕咀嚼時代的膚淺

今天你花了時間與我穿街過巷
城市另一邊會有不同品種嗎？
是昔日曾見過是我幻想的芳香
柔軟肌膚是時日醞釀成有情的懷抱
咬一口，滿嘴成熟的清香
都說沒有了，感謝你陪我繼續尋找

2008

Artichoke

It used to hide its feelings
quite unlike the tomatoes
squirting at you with every bite
or durians divulging
the aroma of power.
The artichoke is subtle,
bringing its own history,
testing one's patience,
artichoke, a little at odds with its time,
looking like a lotus lamp
keeping its own secrets
yet empty of mysteries.
It can't fly, unlike fireworks
blowing up a stretch of sky,
or rockets changing a day's weather.
In silence it sits quietly by the window,
in love with the glamorous yellow flower
gazing at the flower's early morning tears,
her brightening soul stretching at dusk
after the scorching sun is set,
appreciating all her merits
but thinking she would prefer the sunflower
the crab chrysanthemum with claws in every direction.
So the artichoke stays put,
a little slow, a little old-fashioned,
its heavy armory unable to join the world's dance.
It savors the glamour of the surrounding colors
but knows that it takes a particular taste
to appreciate green skin with a rusty edge,

雅芝竹

習慣了把感情收藏
他不像蕃茄那樣
咬破了噴得一身都是
不像榴槤，宣揚強勢的氣味
雅芝竹是含蓄的
他帶着自己的歷史
考驗你的耐性
雅芝竹，有點不合時宜
看來像盞蓮花燈
好似守住私己的教義
放在眼前可沒有什麼神祕
他不會飛翔，也不像煙花
爆破一面天空，像火箭
改變一天的氣候
他沉默地坐在窗邊
默默愛上燦爛的黃花
看見她早晨的淚珠、經歷烈日
在薄暮裏舒展亮麗的靈魂
明白她各種好處
但想她一定更喜歡向日葵
張牙舞爪的蟹爪菊
所以雅芝竹只是默在那裏
他是有點慢，有點老派
沉重的裝甲趕不上世界的舞步
他細味周圍多姿的顏色
可也明白，需要特殊的口味
才會欣賞微帶銹邊的青綠

潮流和標準不斷變化
雅芝竹經過那麼多
知道人情曲折，勢利或善美
他相信自己還是有能力好好去愛
不過就還是老把自己包裹得嚴嚴密密的
不容易看得見雅芝竹青嫩的心
只不過有時一不小心
頭上一下子冒出縷縷鮮藍的花

2008

trends and standards constantly changing.
The artichoke has been through that much,
understands the tribulations of life,
knows the chills and the warmth.
He imagines he still has the ability to love
but nonetheless wraps himself tight.
It's not easy to glimpse the artichoke's soft heart,
only by accident sometimes,
a bunch of fresh blue flowers
grows out from his head.

2008
Translated by the Author with Afaa M. Weaver

Green Salad

naked strands pour layers of time over green threads
freshly washed, bright 'n shiny and crisp
search for a curled leaf in the greasy din
open its perplexing colour to find resentment
listen closely and know sadness—
no longer in love with the colour? the pieces too tough
sit here quietly drinking up life, loneliness
taste this tender leaf, so mild and captivating

yesterday's passion is now an empty seat
as if the purple has rusted into a new colour
swaying shadows are a noise of red-sauce
layer upon layer—and what else is there
sharing a table could mean not sharing the way home
clusters of dew on dawn leaves are worlds apart
banquet blossoms bloom and fade—this we know
carved in gold and jade words can never say it all

knife and fork pick up the strands of age-old entanglements
lean red fat green diluted bitter cabbage
shaggy shoots of bamboo love the yellow pepper
not fond of sweet and glutinous, there's hot and spicy
cloves of human relationships hide you and me
on a road so long oranges taste like durian
separated by acres of corn we meet here again
light and shadow dancing—stop this glass, this wine

shallow plates teach us how to chew deeply
dabs of rouge revive an old-time grandeur
new and upbeat sounds chattering all around
neon lights a thousand leaves as the conversation turns cold
when you speak soundlessly of licorice of almond yellow
an experience from thick to thin is slowly re-tasted
these days, more than ever, I love this fresh bitterness
holding so many broken pieces in no particular order

青菜沙律

青絲　素縷上　澆層層　時間　　　刀叉　牽起　絡絡　前塵糾結
新淨　明麗的　還有　那清爽　　　綠肥紅瘦　給　苦白菜　沖稀
饜膩　喧嘩裏　尋一株　彎捲　　　重疊參差　甘筍　喜歡　黃椒
撥開　詭祕顏色　發現　怨對　　　不愛　甜稠　也可以　愛苦辣
用心　聆聽　明白　那是憂傷　　　瓣瓣　人際關係　掩映　你我
已不愛　五彩嗎　片片　硬脆　　　長長的　路上　柑橘　似榴槤
會心靜坐　喝出　生命　清冷　　　相隔　萬畝玉米　相遇　於此
嚐到　葉嫩　淡薄　令人出神　　　光影　晃盪裏　停下　這杯酒

曾經　情盡意竭　如今　留空　　　淺碟　教我們　也想　嚼深呢
彷彿　紫鏽　蝕出了　新顏色　　　幾層　胭脂　裝扮　舊的排場
虛晃的　影子　醬紅的　喧嘩　　　四周　寒暄　自有　新的高昂
疊疊層層　底下　還有　甚麼　　　霓虹照　千重葉　話語　涼了
同桌　可以　有不同的　方向　　　等你說　無聲的　甘味　杏黃
叢叢黎明　葉露　相隔　萬家　　　經歷　由濃而淡　逐一　咀嚼
盛宴　繽紛　開落　自然知道　　　如今　逐漸　愛苦澀的　清新
金鏤玉刻　言語　不能　盡意　　　包容　種種　破碎　不知秩序

1988

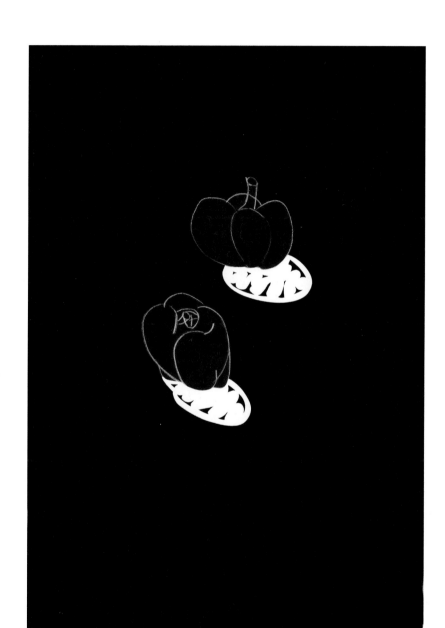

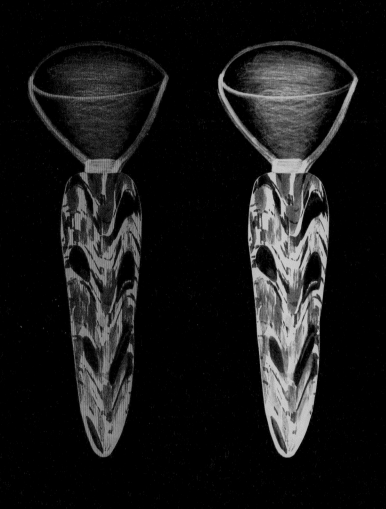

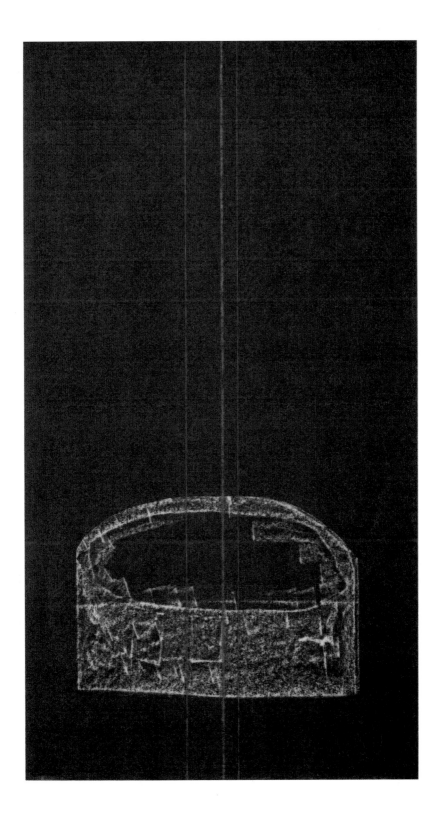

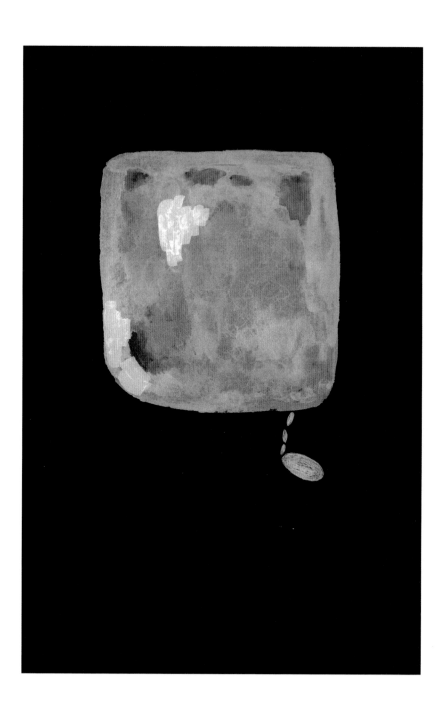

Hainanese Chicken Rice (Singapore Version)

Do I have the best recipe
for blanching chicken in water
for remaking tenderness in a foreign land
consoling parents who drifted over oceans?

Do I have the best recipe
for just the right sauce and ginger dip
for reconciling the taboos of food and language
readjusting to the new rules of the dinner table?

Do I have the best recipe
for rice in chicken broth with just the right texture
for making it less oily, to please the new neighbours,
adapting to a city's diverse appetite?

2002
Translated by the Author

新加坡的海南雞飯

我可有最好的祕方
用沸水把雞浸熟
在異鄉重造故鄉的鮮嫩
安慰飄洋過海的父母？

我可有最好的祕方
調製最美味的醬油和薑茸
調節食物和語言裏的禁忌
適應新的餐桌的規矩？

我可有最好的祕方
把雞湯煮出軟硬適中的熱飯
測試油膩的分寸在異地睦鄰
黏合一個城市裏多元的胃口？

2002

Hap La Gung (Vietnamese Stuffed Snails in Ginger Leaves)

I was picked from a field of water
plucked out
minced
added dried mushrooms, lean meat and onion
salt
fish sauce and pepper
a blade of strange ginger leaf
stuffed
back into my shell
to give me more taste

I was plucked out
removed from
my geography and history
given exotic colors
foreign flavors
added value
higher price
all to place me
into some future
unknown

2002
Translated by the Author

釀田螺

把我從從水田撿起
把我拿出來
切碎了
加上冬菇、瘦肉和洋蔥
加上鹽
魚露和胡椒
加上一片奇怪的薑葉
為了再放回去
我原來的殼中
令我更加美味

把我拿出來
使我遠離了
我的地理和歷史
加上異鄉的顏色
加上外來的滋味
給我增值
付出了昂貴的代價
為了把我放到
我不知道的
將來

2002

Pun Choi (Hong Kong Basin Feast)

Roast rice-duck and pan-fried prawns are always on top
Class order is precisely laid out in the layers
But the poking chopsticks gradually reverse
the prized five-spice chicken and lowly pigskin
The Sung army once sought shelter here in defeat
wolfed down the fishermen's reserves from large wooden basins
dined on the beach in crude circles, with no elegance of the past
Far from the capital, they tried the rural folks' wild flavours.

Unable to stay on top, it all collapses with gradual consumption
Like it or not, there's no escape from touching the colours on the bottom
no way to block the encounter between humble mushroom and rare squid
Inverted relationships taint and affect the purity on top
Nobody can stop the meat juice from trickling down, from allowing
the bottom-most turnip to absorb every flavour in all its sweetness.

2002
Translated by the Author

盆菜

應該有燒米鴨和煎海蝦放在上位
階級的次序層層分得清楚
撩撥的筷子卻逐漸顛倒了
圍頭五味雞與粗俗的豬皮
狼狽的宋朝將軍兵敗後逃到此地
一個大木盆裏吃漁民貯藏的餘糧
圍坐灘頭進食無復昔日的鐘鳴鼎食
遠離京畿的輝煌且試鄉民的野味

無法虛排在高處只能隨時日的消耗下陷
不管願不願意亦難不蘸底層的顏色
吃久了你無法隔絕北菇與排魷的交流
關係顛倒互相沾染影響了在上的潔癖
誰也無法阻止肉汁自然流下的去向
最底下的蘿蔔以清甜吸收了一切濃香

2002

Bibimbap (Korean Stone-grilled Rice)

Myriad vegetables
each with its own beauty
Whose hands are shaking the bellflower,
stringing them into a tune round your neck?
Slice the cucumber into half-moons
dip them in sesame oil
Tenderly massage the lettuce
letting it play a *haegum* melody
Transform the mushrooms into ten long drums
raise a desolate wind among autumn reeds
arrange the bean sprouts and watch them disperse in the din
letting the *daegum* play on the cool dawn
Let the beets tell secrets in their hearts
and dye everybody red
Each beauty its own hidden woe
So many vegetables stirred and heated in one stone basin
alter the rice into a song of blended colour

2002
Translated by the Author

Note:
胡弓 haegum and 長竹笛 daegum
are Korean musical instruments

石鍋拌飯

許許多多的蔬菜
各有各的美麗和驕橫
甚麼樣的一雙手搖響風鈴草
把它掛成一串頸上炫耀的小調
把青瓜切成半個月亮
把月亮蘸點麻油
溫柔地給生菜按摩
讓它發出胡弓的旋律
把冬菇變成十只長鼓
敲出秋天蘆葦間的蕭殺
芽菜姊妹排好又在動亂中拆散
長竹笛合奏黎明的爽涼
讓紅菜頭翻出絃間的祕密
把人家的臉龐染紅
美麗底下有隱藏的悲涼
這麼多的蔬菜交纏的歌舞
在炙熱的石盆上錯折成形
把白飯攪拌成斑駁的七彩

2002

Tom Yum Kung Soup (Thai Hot Soup)

The spiciest is pepper
The spiciest is water

The spiciest her lips
The spiciest your earplugs

The spiciest the official announcements
The spiciest your gossip columns

The spiciest her body
The spiciest his gaze

The spiciest her smell
The spiciest your nose

The spiciest his hot kiss
The spiciest her indifference

The spiciest his nakedness
The spiciest her constant neatness

The spiciest his eyes
The spiciest her moods

The spiciest their basic law
The spiciest our self-censorship

The spiciest her charming dimple
The spiciest when you're vulnerable

The spiciest their language
The spiciest our silence

2002
Translated by the Author

冬蔭功湯

最辣的是辣椒
最辣的是清水

最辣是她的嘴巴
最辣是你的耳塞

最辣是他們的發布
最辣是你們的報道

最辣是她的身體
最辣是他的凝睇

最辣是她的氣味
最辣是你的大鼻

最辣是他的熱吻
最辣是她的冷漠

最辣是他的裸體
最辣是她的整齊

最辣是他的眼睛
最辣是她的心情

最辣是他們的法紀
最辣是我們的顧忌

最辣是她的梨渦
最辣是你的無助

最辣是他們的言語
最辣是我們的無言

2002

Larb (Laos Sticky Rice with Meat)

A cleaver drumming on the chopping board
calls forth our yearning for a warm supper
The meat slowly matures under the pounding
Shredded vegetables grow more complete
Glutinous rice has its own tender charm
holding together all the shattered pieces of the day
Time spent preparing a dish
accumulates into an exquisite harvest

2002
Translated by the Author

老撾菜肉飯

刀在砧板上細切的聲音
呼喚我們期待溫暖的晚飯
肉在琢磨中逐漸成熟
蔬菜撕裂了變得更完整
香草的苦辣帶出魚的鮮美
糯米有它溫柔的魅力
把所有日常的破碎黏合
預備一道菜所花的時間
點點滴滴收穫它的美味

2002

Nasi Lemak (Malaysian Coconut Rice)

Never feeling hungry when you eat it
Never feeling sad

Fewer and fewer people grow rice
Fewer and fewer work the fields

The city develops different tastes
Yet rice always soothes our pain

Feeling full when you eat it
Feeling strong when you have it

Fewer and fewer people sow seeds in Spring
Fewer and fewer harvest in Autumn

Fewer and fewer people grind grain
Fewer and fewer husk rice

The city scars you in seven colours
The rice consoles you in white

Never feeling grief when you eat it
Never feeling rage

Never feeling lost when you have it
Never going astray

The city develops various melancholies
Will rice hold together the shards of our beliefs?

2002
Translated by the Author

馬來椰醬飯

吃了永不會飢餓　　　　　　城市帶給你七色的疤痕
吃了永不會憂傷　　　　　　米飯給你白色的安慰

插秧的人愈來愈少了　　　　吃了永不會悲傷
種稻的人愈來愈少了　　　　吃了永不會激憤

城市發展出不同的口味　　　吃了永不會迷路
米飯永遠中和我們的辛酸　　吃了永不會失落

吃了感到充實　　　　　　　城市發展出不同的憂傷
吃了就有氣力　　　　　　　米飯黏合我們離散的信仰

隨着季節播種　　　　　　　2002
隨着季節收割的人
愈來愈少了

隨着季節去打穀
隨着季節去曬穀

磨穀的人愈來愈少了
舂米的人愈來愈少了

Nasi Kuning (Indonesian Yellow Rice)

India brought over spices and curry
Arabian shish kebab became satay
The Dutch devoured nutmeg and cumin
Chinese fled with black beans and vegetable seeds
Soy sauce landed here grew sweet
Numerous islands dot the dining table's coastline
Nobody can colonize spices

Turmeric dyes my fingers yellow
Padan leaves give off their strong scent
Fiery chili peppers refuse to kowtow
Hot as volcanic lava
Rugged as ocean rock. Only

Rice is our common language
Rice our consoling mother
Rice encompassing all colours
Rice soothing a stomach's old wounds

2002
Translated by the Author

印尼黃飯

印度帶來了香料和咖喱
阿拉伯人的串燒變成沙爹
荷蘭人覬覦豆蔻和茴香
中國人背着豆豉和菜籽逃難
豉油遠道而來定居在這裏變甜
餐桌的海岸線上無數小島
大家都沒法把香料殖民

黃薑染黃了我手指頭
香蘭葉總有濃郁的香氣
辣椒火爆拒絕向任何人低頭
火山溶岩那麼熾烈
海岸巉礁那種嶙峋，只有⋯⋯

米飯是我們共通的言語
米飯是我們安慰的母親
米飯包容不同的顏色
米飯燙貼腸胃裏舊日的傷痕

2002

Jongjong ju (Korean New Wine)

Undergoing changes
yet uncertain of its identity
Slowly precipitating shape
in a pale white form
Milk or chilled soup?
Tiny bubbles on the surface
scooped out from the vortex, a previous life's sorghum
The many possibilities of a pre-form state

transforming into bright red leaves
into elegant gingkoes
gloomy tunnels
fatal explosions
wintry melodies of love
woeful ballads
self-destructive leaps from cliffs
aspired ascensions

Seasoned men drinking wine
distinguish many tastes
Once there were so many possibilities at hand
The face of the world still fresh
Elegant curves floating along the milky white
So many ripples in crystal-clear water
choosing to become wine or vinegar
Let's savor this wonderful liquid of ambiguous tastes

6/11/2004, drinking with Fujii, Yamaguchi, and Lam
Translated by the Author

新濾酒

剛剛經歷新的變化
還未肯定自己的身份
點滴濾下形成
淡白的形態
是牛乳還是冷湯呢？
臉上還有小小的泡泡
漩渦裏撈出前生的大米
未形成的狀態裏有許多可能

變成鮮艷的紅葉
變成體面的銀杏
變成陰暗的地道
變成致命的爆炸
變成冬天的戀曲
變成悲情的高歌
變成躍崖的自毀
變成得道的昇天

上了年紀的人在喝酒
喝出了許多味道
一度眼前有那麼多可能
世界的臉孔還是那清新
乳白裏盪着動人的弧線
清澈的水裏有那麼多波紋
可以選擇變酒還是變醋
且賞模棱的味道煥發的美漿

06/11/2004　晚與藤井、山口及林教授共飲

Banten in Bali

A small basin made from palm leaves
carrying flowers, rice
a bit of fruit and salt
sprinkled with holy water
placed at the door as sacrifice

To the Gods of the mountain crests
to the evil spirits of the ocean depths
Praying for the protection of all we have
from the disasters of volcanoes and earthquakes
from the torture of epidemics
from the explosions that kill so many
praying for tourists to return unafraid

We respect gods and fear evil spirits
Many footsteps trigger hidden currents
many dogs tread on buried secrets
the blue shadows of the walls
When one protects
one is Vishnu
When one destroys
one is Surya

That stretch of red earth
with its unpredictable lives and deaths
Shimmering streaks of light and shade
in the depths of the forests
in the depths of our hearts
A small palm leaf boat
ferrying our respect and fear
trembling on the waves

2002
Translated by the Author

峇里的祭品

用棕櫚葉造成小盆　　　　　那一片紅色的土地
承載了花朵、米飯　　　　　上有無常的生死
一點點的水果和鹽　　　　　那閃爍不定的片片光影
灑上聖水　　　　　　　　　在森林的最裏面
放在門前獻祭　　　　　　　在我們心的最深處
　　　　　　　　　　　　　小小一葉棕櫚的小舟
向住在山頂的神靈　　　　　承載了敬畏與恐懼
向住在海底的惡靈　　　　　在波濤上顛簸
祈求保佑我們所有的一切
免於火山和地震的災害
免於傳染病的凌虐　　　　　2002
免於令數百人喪命的爆炸
祈求遊客再來不害怕

我們敬畏神明但也懼怕惡靈
人的腳步牽動潛伏的暗流
狗的四足踐踏誰的祕密
那一片藍色的牆影
當他保護事物
他是毘濕奴
當他破壞時
他是濕婆

President Li's Menu

the president likes an appetizer called Long Life Lucky-Dip:
lilies plucked in full bloom, oven dried and mixed with mackerel
tribute kale from south and west, dressed and served cold
all the clacking duck-tongues spiced and stewed in a bowlful of gravy

in the prime of life he loved rich and heavy flavours
getting on in years now, he's had to lighten up
for instance, take some boiled milkfish and
match it with black beans that stimulate digestion

for him, like every senior citizen,
ordinary soy sauce is wrong
so simmer black fermented bean stock to bring out the taste of soy
in lobster there's too much cholesterol
so substitute with sea cucumber

he likes fresh and tasty fish-lips simmered with shiitake
easy for an older man to suck and chew upon
all nuts must be ground and steamed until soft
then scattered over winter melon like a gauzy curtain
his sense of taste may be a little slow, but texture is more important

he goes back more and more, back to his own bailiwick
he likes country-style pickled radishes and dried cucurbit flowers
and can make his own *bidaibo* rice cakes
but bland and uneventful won't always be to his taste
at some point he'll need to spice things up again

1999
Translated by Brian Holton

總統的菜單

總統喜歡爽口前菜「福祿壽」
把盛放的曇花摘下烘乾伴着鯖魚
把各方蠻夷進貢來的貢菜涼拌
把所有喧囂的鴨舌頭拔下來鹵成一盆

在春秋盛年愛吃濃味
現在年紀大了不免清淡一點
比方把煮過的虱目魚
配上有助腸胃消化的烏豆

像所有高齡的人一樣
不適合用食用醬油
就用高湯燉豆豉帶出醬油香味
龍蝦的膽固醇太高了
就用海參代替吧

還喜歡鮮美的魚唇燉花菇
適合老年人慢慢咀嚼
所有堅果都得磨碎蒸爛
用來覆蓋冬瓜如朦朧的窗紗
味覺雖較緩慢口感是最重要的

愈來愈回歸鄉土了
喜歡鄉下的菜莆和葫蘆花乾
也能自己用米造米苔目
只是嘴裏有時不甘平淡
也來那麼的辣它一下

1999

A Taste of Asia

The jar you sent had just arrived, stood still unopened,
When the grim tidings blew in from the grey clouds
North of your coast. The earth's contractions
Had brought forth a tsunami. A hotel swallowed in an instant.
A train thrown from its tracks, continuing derailed, driverless
On a journey from this life to the next.
The ocean suddenly overhead. Human lives
Oilslick-black, flotsam doors, provisions adrift, homeless . . .

I open the tightly sealed jar. Pickled garlic.
What is this taste? A bitterness
Buried deep in layers of mud? A harshness of trees broken apart?
A stench of ocean, shattered coral, fish floating belly-up?
What does it speak of, your message, wafted my way this sunny afternoon?
Of something brewing in the dark? Of something growing in turmoil?
Of pity and cruelty, glimpsed in the heaving motions of nature?
Can a drop of sweetness temper the infinite brine of this world's woe!

2004
Translated by John Minford

亞洲的滋味

剛收到你寄來的瓶子，還未打開
沒想到，隨灰雲傳來了噩耗
沿你們的海岸線北上，地殼的震動
掀起海嘯，一所酒店在剎那間淹沒
一列火車沖離軌道，無人駕駛
從今生出軌闖入來世的旅程
海水突然淹過頭頂：油膩而污黑的
生命、飄浮的門窗、離家的食物……

我打開密封的瓶子，嚐不出
這醃製的蒜頭是怎樣一種滋味
是泥層中深埋的酸澀、樹木折斷的焦苦
還是珊瑚折盡魚肚翻白的海的鹹腥？
從陽光普照的午後傳來，你可是想告訴我
如何在黑暗中醞釀，在動亂中成長
千重輾軋中體會大自然的悲憫與殘酷？
如何以一點甘甜調理大地人世無邊酸楚？

2004

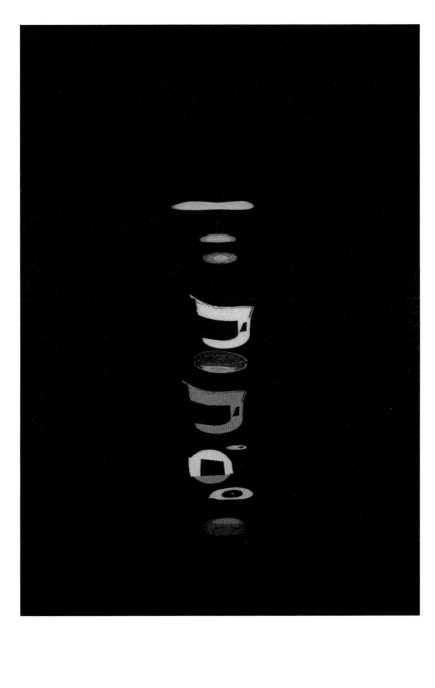

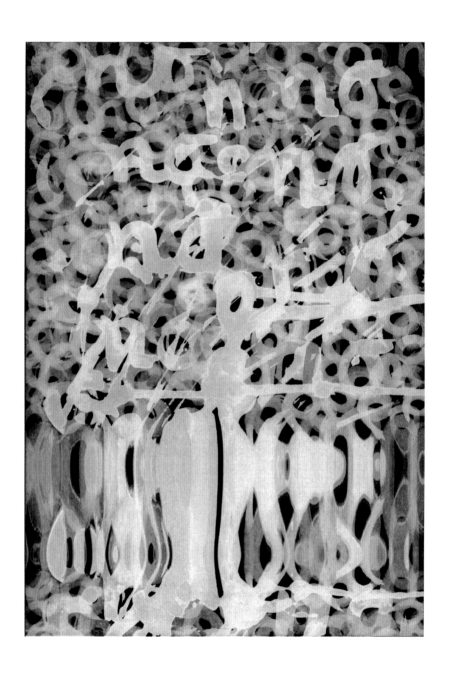

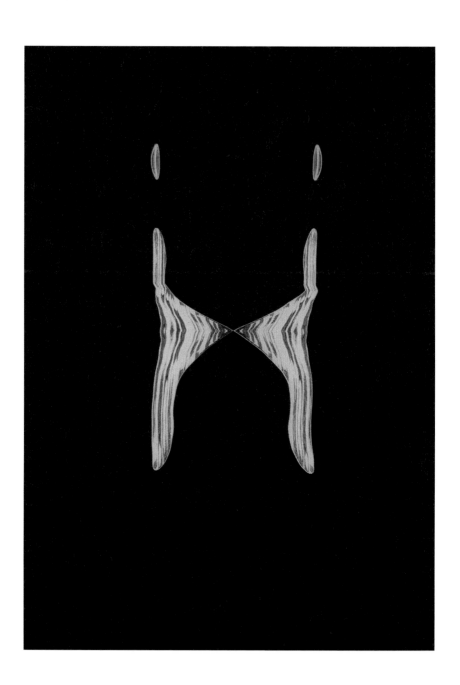

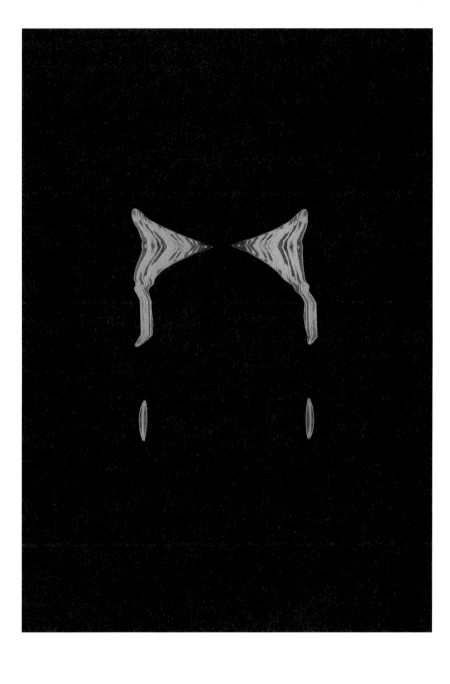

Fourteen Chairs

Your cushion receives glory's rise and fall in a magic mirror
Mirages flashing, tycoons conjuring luxury high rises
Gaze into the train station that is gone, into the Long March further gone,
History sits with Earth, witnesses its constant layering of glaze.

As a chair, you have received white-collar workers who sit dully all day long,
You have consoled vagabonds, saved runaways from the streets,
Given respite to refugees of war. Why not open your arms for more?
Let spirits of migrating birds rest here. The Flying Dutchman has returned to the garden.

Twilight has fallen on the clock tower, from the concert hall fragments of music
Slow down the hurried pedestrians, quicken their numbed nerves.
Another person's creation, what is he trying to tell us?

You are depressed by the prolonged strain, but if you don't stand
How can people lean on you? Finally, I see you struggle to stand
In rain and fog, with last summer's setback and hope, to arrive at your rightful place.

2004
Translated by the Author with Michelle Yeh and Afaa M. Weaver

十四張椅子

你微軟的靠墊承受住幻鏡中興奮與頹唐的起伏
蜃樓隱現，商賈善舞的長袖幻變廣廈三千
眺望已不存在的火車站，想像更遠的長征
歷史坐在那裏與大地見証人間不斷窰變的斑痕窰

你若是一張椅子，承受過整日呆坐工作的白領
安慰城市裏失意的流浪人，收容街頭的浪蕩少年
在戰火間讓難民休憩，何妨開放包容更多
避冬鳥兒的靈魂來過冬，園裏有倦飛歸來的荷蘭人

鐘樓已是黃昏，音樂廳裏傳來樂章的斷片
挽住行人匆忙的腳步，撩撥麻木的神經
那另一人的創作，想告訴我們的是甚麼？

長期承受筋肉酸痛易令人消沉，但你若不站起來
又怎可以扶持他人？我終見你帶着去夏的希望連着挫折
在冷雨濕霧中顫危危站起，攀援抵達自己的位置

2004

An American's First Visit to Hong Kong
in the Mid-nineteenth Century

1.

A friend complains that the weather here causes clothes to mold

Protection is needed from the Sun! Each time you walk through a door,
    Chinese servants are there with an umbrella

No one knows what to do on scorching hot days

In the end they always remain inside the spacious, winding verandas,
    sleeping away the afternoons lost in dreams

2.

On the big roads brought over by the British, locals shave their heads,
    weave rattan, and repair tools

Long-braided men hawk their goods, hanging strange flattened ducks
    and salty fish in their stalls

Foreign sailors callously knock over a learned old scholar on the street

Pushing open a local resident's door, they cause a fearful commotion

3.

Everyone is talking about last night's Coolie melee, how they used
    bamboo sticks to bash each other's skulls

Bamboo sheds surround new buildings on the streets. A new face causes
    the old face to grow old

British arrogance is concentrated in the Central District, the sovereigns
    gaze at the harbor but only see

Kowloon Peninsula, rumors of a mysteriously disappeared foreign devil
    spread from its labyrinth alleys

4.

They find it strange that we do not want to ride in sedan chairs, carried
    by four servants to the Mid-Levels woods

Where there are strangely named longans, lychees and pomelos, I am
    afraid the mountain road is steep

The higher up the more desolate it gets, I believe peculiar anteaters and
    poisonous snakes are there

Coolies walk in front carrying lanterns, armed police wait for suspicious
    movements each bit of the way

十九世紀中葉初訪香港的一位美國人

一、

一位朋友埋怨這裏的天氣令衣服長出霉黴

要提防毒太陽！每當你走近大門，總有中國僕人

舉起一把大傘，炎熱的日子大家不知該做甚麼才好

到頭來總是留在寬敞的迴廊上睡亂夢的午覺

二、

英國人帶來了大街，人們在剃頭、編藤器、修理工具

長辮男子在叫賣，攤檔上掛着奇怪的壓扁的臘鴨和鹹魚

也有外國水手放浪撞倒路上的老師宿儒

推開一扇民居的門，引起一陣驚惶的喧嘩

三、

大家都在說昨夜苦力的混戰，用竹桿互相毆打頭顱

路上圍上竹棚的新建築。一張新臉孔令一張舊臉孔變老

英國人的虛榮都集中在中區，君臨海港眺望只望見

九龍半島，迷宮般巷道傳來「番鬼」神祕失蹤的謠言

四、

他們奇怪我為甚麼不想坐轎，由四個僕人抬上半山林叢

那兒有怪名字的龍眼、荔枝和柚子，我怕山路陡斜

愈上愈冷清，想那兒有異樣的穿山甲和毒蛇

苦力舉着燈籠走在前面，隔不遠一個警察武裝以待異動

五、

突然一陣狂風暴雨，把宴罷的我們趕回去酒店內盤桓

不停地敲窗推門要進來，那狂暴的怪獸我們看不見臉

盛裝男女黎明看見窗外傾倒的大蕉樹，滯留室內我們還安全

灣畔小船卻失蹤了，正在打撈屍體，外面總是說不出的危險

5.

After our banquet a violent rainstorm suddenly causes us to rush back to
the hotel to idle about

That violent, mythical beast whose face we cannot see incessantly taps at
the window and pushes the door

At dawn splendidly attired men and women see the uprooted banana
tree, cooped up inside we are still safe

The small boat in the harbour is missing and they are salvaging for
corpses, unspeakable dangers always out there

6.

We go to the lobby and listen to a sermon, the educated priest looks out
the window and seems to see

A canvas of beautiful scenery from the future: a pure white new ship sets
sail for each corner of the world! Opium?

It's part of the past, but Chinese and Westerners from different lands
admire each other, people are proud living here!

Brethren of James Legge, this is all well and good, but it really is a bit
too damn optimistic!

1998
Translated by Glen Steinman

六、
我們到大會堂聽演講，這位有學問的神父望出窗外彷彿看見
一幅將來的美景：潔白的新船啟航到世界各地去！鴉片？
已盡成陳跡，華洋雜處卻互相欣賞，人們以生活在此地為榮！
這敢情好，但真是他媽的樂觀呢，理雅各弟兄！

1998

In Response to Cecil Clementi

I gaze from the foot of the mountain
and espy
not a single firefly
steaming by,
not a single star
gleaming in the sky,
no fairy lights on an earthly paradise,
But a Special Economic Zone
lit up in a blaze of Japanese neon
dazzling the eye.
See how hard I have to try
to squeeze myself into your foreign rhyme!
For years I've had to stammer like this
in your borrowed tongue!
So what do I feel now? Indifference?
Or a strange nostalgia? Now that you are going—gone—
Images flit past
a-sparkle a-flash
An older rhapsody, an older rhetoric
  takes the measure of us
  trusses us up in the strong calligraphy of tradition
  condescends to dribble a drop of casual scholar's ink
and there we are—cultural waifs—
  no match for your aspirations
  hearing all this fulsome praise
In utter seriousness, without a snigger
  we watch silently by the deathbed

悼逝去的
——和金文泰香港詩

我從山腳下仰望已經看不見星空
太燦爛了日本電器廣告牌一重重
不會以為這是蓬萊這經濟的特區
費盡思量勉強步和你異鄉的韻律
多年來你的言語總令我結結巴巴
是冷漠還是傷感呢對於你的離去？

眼前閃過一列又一列璀璨的意象
猶似漢賦雄辯滔滔把我們來丈量
書寫我們在傳統的鐵劃銀勾之中
灑落一點墨跡，是被棄的文字孤兒
不如你的期望，聆聽世代人的善頌
我們沒有竊笑，默對彌留的病床

完了嗎？不，消逝又倖存，輾轉反側
商人與士兵共舞取悅抑嘲諷星辰？
在言語買賣裏也做過歡快的生意
大家習慣了在僵硬的形式裏舒伸
霧島迷湖連同巍巍崑崙泰山壓頂
把寶珠埋葬，這樣就完了嗎？也許？不？

1997

An ending? No!

A passing, a surviving, a tossing and a turning—

Will the merchants and soldiers dance together for pleasure,

or will they mock the starry consummation?

The commerce of words continues brisk;

Everyone has grown accustomed to moving

within the old, stiff format.

And there they lie

Your misty isle, the haze-wrapped waters of Albion,

The towering peaks of *our* Cathay,

Bearing down on us,

Crushing, burying the pearl—

An ending? Perhaps?

Not

1997
Translated by John Minford

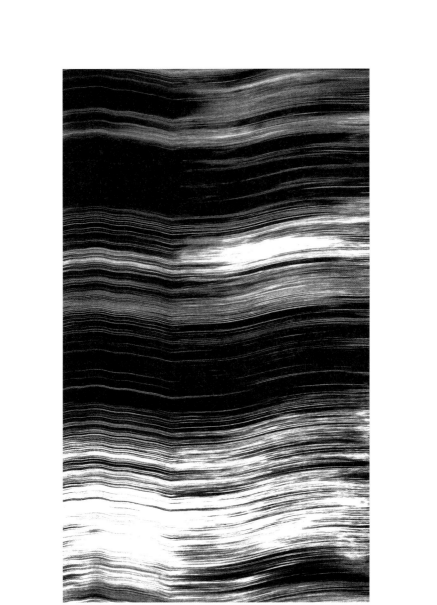

Lin Huiyin and Liang Sicheng in Search
of an Ancient Shanxi Temple

A long time ago, you set out to explore
a temple renowned by many. You hired a car,
rode mules, and finished on foot, trekking across
rickety tracks of rusted narrow railroad built by warlords.
Though there were those who made the course impassable,
you reached the pagoda fatigued, disturbed
to discover that over and over, violence and ignorance had gutted
the heart of the building, majestic murals
scraped off and sold to peddlers of cultural relics,
leaving behind only a broken-hearted blank wall.

On this day a great door opened for you.
At dusk you discerned the grandeur and antiquity,
checking for dates along the beams.
Determined to decode the mind behind ancient designs,
you climbed the dark attic, tried to use modern light to illuminate
the thick black stink and decay of a thousand-year slumber.
Were you sure that you'd uncover the framework that we'd dreamed of?
Or would it just be piled-up bat corpses and insects
gnawing at so many years of people's back-breaking efforts
while you unfurled layer after layer of sediment in pursuit of elegance?

So much stuck in the sleep-land of human neglect,
but at this instant, your vision rescued archaic lines
from numbness, guided us to gaze up at eaves and brackets.
After a dazed millennium, you detected the wisdom of the past,
sought the logic and symmetry of timber structures,
astute observations and precise measurements
all recorded in a book,
unaware that at the same time in the far-off capital,
enemy troops had reignited the flames of war and razed new houses,
savages intent on annihilating more civilizations.

1999–2000
Translated by Jennifer Feeley

林徽因梁思成尋見山西的古寺

在那以前你們曾經動程前往
許多聽說過的寺廟，僱一輛車
乘着騾，最後徒步走過軍閥建的
東歪西倒的生銹窄軌鐵路
儘管總有人令通路變成不可能
疲乏地抵達一座寶塔，心情矛盾
但見時間、暴力和愚昧反覆刪削
心中的建築，秀麗的壁畫
剷掉賣給文物販子去了
只餘下一堵傷心的空牆

今天這高大的門登時就給你打開了
你在昏暗裏辨識它的雄偉與古老
你們沿着橫樑去尋上面的日期
想要揣摩那遠古的建造的心意
攀上黑暗閣樓，嘗試用現代燈光燭照
沉睡了千年的厚厚黑黑的髒亂與腥臭
你們肯定那底下有我們嚮往的造型？
抑或只有蝙蝠積聚的屍體，還有蟲豸
咬嚙盡多少年來人們的心血
更撥開這層層淤積來尋見優雅？

許多東西在人們的忽略中沉睡了
但在這一刻，你的目光從麻木中救出
古老的線條，帶我們仰望斗拱和屋簷
在千年的昏沉底下看出曾有過的智慧
你追隨木結構的理智與平衡
那些靈巧的心思，你們細細丈量
在一本本子上把一切記下來
不知道這時在遠方的京城
敵軍重燃戰火燒掉新的房舍
野蠻將要毀滅更多文明

1999–2000

Still Life

At the beginning, there was someone sitting on the chair
At the beginning, there was someone sitting at the table
At the beginning, there was someone watering a plant
At the beginning, there was someone looking up from the books

Where have they all gone now?

The one who danced to the music
The one who liked eating noodles
The one who liked drinking plain water
The one who wore a hat to keep off the sun

Where have they all gone now?

Someone who wanted to have a good talk with you
Someone who wanted to hold your hand tight
Someone who wanted to sing loud with you
To look at the sky together with you

Where have they all gone now?

Turned into one who shared a drink of water with total strangers
Turned into one who went on a hunger strike for what he believes in
Turned into one who dissuaded armed police with tears in his eyes
Turned into one who fended off bullets meant for friends

Where have they all gone now?

Squashed to pieces
Riddled with bullets
Blown into sand
Scattered as dust

靜物

本來有人坐在椅上
本來有人坐在桌旁
本來有人給一盆花澆水
本來有人從書本中抬起頭來

現在他們到哪兒去了？

那個隨着音樂起舞的人
那個喜歡吃麵條的人
那個喜歡喝白開水的人
那個戴頂帽子擋陽光的人

現在他們到哪兒去了？

變成一個分水給陌生人喝的人
變成一個為信仰而停止進食的人
變成一個含着眼淚勸告武警的人
變成一個為朋友擋去子彈的人

現在他們到哪兒去了？

輾成了碎片
撞成了彈孔
吹成了風砂
撒成了灰塵

現在他們到哪兒去了？

變成了你我身畔永遠的影子
變成了我們每日的陽光和空氣
變成了生活裏的盆花和桌椅
變成了我們總在讀着的那本書

1989

Where have they all gone now?

Turned into the constant shadows at our sides
Turned into the sun and air of our days
Turned into the plants and furniture in our lives
Turned into the book we read over and over

1989
Translated by the Author

Conversation Among the Ruins

It always comes down to this. We meet in the wilds among the rank weeds and cobble up a room of our own brick by brick, drum up a few essential furnishings, fashion a vestige of decorum, forge the feeling of home.

Then, pillar by pillar, the walls fall without a sound; windows disappear from sight; stairs and gardens are gobbled up for no reason we can discern; and even street signs and shingles dissolve in the twilight. It's all too familiar to us—we're so adept at deciphering the symbols—and yet, even as the wind rises at nightfall and the ruins become distant, we feel the oncoming chill of early autumn.

When the wilderness comes between us and we begin to drift apart, once again, even as I feel the soft but reassuring tablecloth lying beneath the palm of my hand, it begins to vanish like so much wizardry. So too the coffee we drank at breakfast, the fruit we regaled on at noon, the configuration of the fish's skeleton we marveled over, the trivialities in the morning paper that we could not help but scorn. I see you gradually fade away: first your mouth, then your nose, then your eyes.

From the very beginning, it has all come down to this. I find myself flopped out in some hollow in the wilds, suit completely rumpled. Come sunup I work; come nightfall I rest. I move about from place to place in search of water and fresh forage. The bric-a-brac of a lifetime strewn among the ruins of old abodes, never to be retrieved. That sofa you so comfortably sink into instructs you to carefully adjust the tick-tock of the clock, that familiar music which now gathers around you like a throng of old friends . . .

Before it's gone for good, I try to recollect our long conversation over the dinner table and I wonder: what was it we talked about?

1994
Translated by Jennifer Feeley

廢墟中的對話

總是這樣的。 我們在莽莽荒野會面，我們為自己砌好一所房間，
添置一些必需的家具， 鋪排一些殘餘的風俗，營造一份家的
感覺。

然後，逐漸的，牆壁緩緩無聲地塌落，窗戶消失了， 樓梯和花園
不知被甚麼吞沒了， 路牌和門牌在暮色中溶化了。 所有那些讓
我們感到熟悉，賴以辨識的符號，在新起的晚風中離我們遠去，
但覺一片新涼。

等到荒野進入我們之間， 我們只好再度飄泊， 各走各的路。 我
感到柔軟而實在的桌布在我的手掌下面逐漸隱形， 好像魔術一
樣。 連同我們早晨喝過的咖啡，中午吃過的水果， 我們欣賞過
的一副魚骨的形狀， 鄙視過的報紙上的 膚淺的言詞。 我看着你
逐漸消失，先是你的嘴巴， 然後是鼻子， 然後是眼睛。

到頭來總是這樣的。我發現自己睡在荒野的凹坳裏，衣服滿是縐
紋。 日出而作，日入而息。 逐水草而居。 生活裏有許多東西散
落在以前安居的那些家裏， 再也沒法找回來。 那些讓你舒適地
靠着的座椅， 教你好好安排秩序的時鐘， 那些像親切圍坐的朋
友一樣的音樂。

然後我嘗試去追記， 在這一切消失以前， 在晚餐的桌旁， 我們
曾經久久地傾談過的， 我們談的是甚麼呢？

1994

50 Gladstone Avenue

Dear Holly and Ka-sing:
Thanks for inviting me to the opening
of your new gallery. My flight was on time
but two months too soon: 48–50 Gladstone
is still under renovation. Never mind
Our hearts are witness to each other's milestones

Scientific time is not always in sync with our own
Glitches happen, as sometime ago I tried to contact
your state-of-the-art computers. So avant-garde
they preferred self-perfection to conversation

Just as well, isn't it? The past
dismantled, laid out on the floor
Power-cutters cut old connections to make new links
A house in a state of openness:
Wood floor, dare to expose its holey heart
Divisions and doors of protection, yet to be set up

We find our footprints in vintage dust
We look out from the vantage of incompletion:
From the 2nd floor, we perceive
tomorrow's 3rd floor, and yesterday's basement

Started out looking for some storage space along the street
Ended up with a three-story gallery. Fun
can become a responsibility, a heaviness
So many rooms: one to chase out melancholy
one to endure pain from illness, one made esoteric
by *feng shui* and ghosts, another for the family
where children grew

吉石大道五十號

親愛的家昇與楚喬
多謝你們邀請我來參加
新畫廊的開幕禮，航機依時抵達
卻早了兩個月，吉石路四十八、五十號
還在進行裝修工程，沒關係，我們在心中
互相見証彼此生命中的重要時刻

儘管科學的時間並不一定與我們同步
總有參差，就像之前我整天嘗試跟你先進的
電腦系統溝通，但它們太先進了
獨自完善自己，並不情願與我對話。

就這樣不也很好嗎？過去都拆散
分佈在地板的不同區域
電掣切斷舊的糾纏，重新建立新的連繫
房子正處於一種開放的狀態
地板不怕坦露了心中的窟洞
屏障和防禦的門戶有待完成

我們從昔日的灰塵裏發現自己的鞋印
我們從不完整的狀態中張望
卻提供了更好的角度，從二樓
透視未來的三樓，回顧地下的昨天

原先沿街尋找看中儲物的小室
沒想到要連起三層的畫廊，從嬉笑開始
也可以變成責任，夠沉重的
這麼多個不同的房間：在其中一間放逐傷感
在另一間忍受疾病的痛切，一間裏有
幽靈和風水的玄祕，另一間是
子女成長的家常

Old rooms torn down for new configurations
We rock climb on the floor, sail across the ceiling
Tightrope above the sink, headstand on the windowsills
In each room we perform acrobatics for housewarming

Rid of the past (but keep one
elegant front door) to better enter the future?
Each day's progress chips the blueprint in the heart
A different city renovates with different speed and prices
The weighing and measuring and balancing—
A hardship in the making. Will the critic friend from the island
understand, in the end, good art isn't necessarily ironic?

To change wind's direction is hard, in any place
Nomads, disappointed, keep chasing water and grass
As words become monsters, pitching their tents on the web
We communicate in digital language, but don't we also hear
the slow murmuring of our past?

Take the windows and odds and ends for a rich box of art
Then we'll have new shows forever
In front of lenses, murky or sharp
You are the site where great events once happened

When you move the mouse
You are the flowing water of distant imagination
You are the red-white-blue bag carrying the most junk
You are the accents of men and women, the young and the old

What's impossible in this room
Take it to another room
Play your magic. Keep playing
Always carry your roomful of boxes:
One disappeared, a new one invented

2006   Translated by Luo Hui

原來的房間拆去又組成新的圖案
我們在地板上攀石，風帆航過天花板
在水碗上走單桿，在窗緣倒豎蔥
不同的房間裏我們表演的雜技沒有冷場

要把一切過去拆掉（還是要保留
一扇優雅的大門）以便更好地移進未來？
每天看工程的進展總跟心中的藍圖互有齟齬
在不同城市裝修工程有不同的進度與價錢
在逐漸成形的艱困中，衡量如何
把握分寸，不知小島上藝評的朋友到頭來
可會明白：好的藝術不見得就是反諷？

要轉移一個地方的風向談何容易
失望的游牧逐水草而居
當文字變成怪獸，在網上搭起帳蓬
大家用數碼化的語言溝通，卻好似
又聽見了昔日遲緩的耳語？

把窗子連同雜物看成一個豐富的盒子藝術
那就永遠有新的展覽
不管面對朦朧或尖銳的鏡頭
你是大事曾經在此發生的現場

當你移動撥鼠
你是遠方想像的水流
你是攜帶最多雜物的紅白藍膠袋
你是男女老幼的鄉音

不能在這個房間產生的
就在另一個房間完成吧
你們在玩魔術，一直玩下去
隨身帶着許多盒子的房間
一個消失了又變出一個新的

2006

A Haunted House in Berlin

The room is haunted—the woman downstairs told me
she heard footsteps creaking on the stairs
I'm not afraid, I remember how
his expressions gradually turned strange

All those pasts coming back to visit us
those flattened and distorted images in the mirror—it doesn't look like
they're out to harm anyone, their desperate attempts to talk to you
are just to tell you life had been unjust

At one time there were secret tunnels in the city
and sentry posts in winter, they won't easily
be swept away by the brandishing arm of the crane
From the shopping arcade of our desires

a self returns from a foreign land to knock at the door, in his eyes
an expression we find familiar and strange—
Still there? The words I scribbled down
have turned suddenly into signs I cannot decipher

Demons and monsters of our own making are back
to ensnare us, we try but cannot accept today's
love. The remnants of our blurred memories
call us in a whisper amidst flickering shadows in the city

Shall we stand by the window every morning to embrace old wounds?
Or watch old houses on fashionable streets being torn down
leaving not a trace? How does one rebuild the ruins?
We shall have to live with our ghosts

2000
Translated by Martha Cheung

柏林的鬼屋

房子裏有鬼，樓下女人告訴我
聽見樓梯上腳步的聲響
我卻並不害怕，我記得
他的臉容如何逐漸變為奇異

那些過去回來尋見我們
鏡中壓扁的扭曲形象，不見得
要傷害誰，竭力向你說話
是想你終於明白他的冤枉

城市裏曾有祕密的隧道
冬天的哨崗，不容易
被揮舞的吊臂所抹平
我們慾望商場下一個異鄉的

自己回來敲門，他有我們
認識又不認識的眼神──
還在那兒嗎？是我寫下的文字
突然變成無法辨識的符號

我們自己製造的魅魎回來
糾纏我們，無法接受今日的
情愛。過去模糊記憶的頹垣
在城市幢幢陰影裏低喚我們

每個早晨從窗子擁抱老傷疤？
抑或看時新大街上舊房子拆得
不留痕跡？怎從廢墟裏翻新？
我們將要學習如何與鬼魂相處

2000

House in the Valley

Rising at dawn I stroll to the empty space
        behind the house;
I see
        a hammock slung between trees,
        a little sauna shed.

Skirting the house I reach another terrace,
        another door;
A staircase leading to yet another hidden corner,
        ragged creepers rambling
        along the builder's heartlines.

Thirty years ago a young hippy dreamed
        of being a shepherd,
        somewhere beyond the dusty world;
He decided to rebuild this ruined sheep-pen,
        keeping the old stone stairs
        To who-knows-where.
Ancient fossils jut from the steps,
        dragon bones,
        leading to an upper room
        suspended in the void,
An infinite space
        awaiting the fullness of time.

The new master has added Chinese roof tiles.
Here, in the vineyards of the Midi,
        he translates tales of fox-spirits
        from the distant Chinese hills.
Today we sit together outside in the courtyard
        drinking tea,
        his books piled high on the table.

At dusk I watch the last rays of the sunset
        gild the hilltops beyond the garden wall.

峽谷中的房子

晨起信步走到屋後的空地
看林間掛的吊床、暖浴的木屋

繞屋而行看見了另一個小小的露台
另一道門，樓梯通向另一個暗角
參差的菱角隨建者的心思轉形

三十年前一個年輕的嬉皮想在世外牧羊
要把廢棄的羊欄脫胎換骨
　　　　　　　　　　　保留了不知通往那兒的階級
卵石砌出了龍骨
　　　　憑空添了閣樓
　　　　　　　　　　無窮的空間有待年月來填充

如今的主人又再添了中國的簷瓦
在南法葡萄的夜晚翻譯山東的狐仙
今日書成桌上，一眾圍坐屋外喝茶

黃昏在花園裏望見牆外山頂的餘暉
畫葡萄的孩子會長大，睿智的長者
期待歲月下一輪豐盛的收穫

太陽很好，今年的雨水有點不夠
豪雨的時候屋子又會水淹了
「有人去通渠了嗎？」
女主人打點晚餐
　　　　　　　　挪動桌椅的坐向
等房子如好酒醞釀成熟可真不容易

One day the child painting grapes
> Will be a man.
The wise elders
> wait for the rich harvest
> to ripen on the wheel of time.

The sun is so fine.
> This year the rains were too few;
And then the floods came,
> And the house was awash.
"Can someone unblock the drain?"
The lady of the house prepares the evening meal,
> Sets out table and chairs.
How hard it is,
> Waiting for a house to mature,
> Like a vintage.

That night I slept beside the grand piano,
Happy to have found a corner
> To lay my weary traveller's head.

Strolling at dawn up the hillside behind the house
I turn to gaze at the row of trees,
> At the windbreak protecting
> Your home.

2006
Translated by John Minford

晚上我睡在大鋼琴的旁邊
高興旅途中作客有個憩息的角落

早晨信步從屋後走上山
回望山谷裏擋風的樹叢蔽佑了你的房子

2006

Cityscape

The city is always the colour of neon
Secret messages hidden there
The pity is only, you're wearing a mask
No way to know if it's you that's speaking

Fruit from many different places
Each with its own tale to tell
In newly dressed shop windows
Che Guevara rhymes with the latest in shoes

In your little cafes I bump into
Friends I haven't seen in years
Between pickles and green tea porridge
A cup of tea has drunk away a lifetime

Have any spare change?
There are plenty of gods on sale in the market
She cherishes the memory of her last life's rouge
He likes the celadon green of city dust

So sing me a song
On the winding midnight street
Yesterday and us, we've come face to face
But however we try, we can never recall today

2003
Translated by Brian Holton

城市風景

城市總有霓虹的燈色
那裏有隱密的訊息
只可惜你戴起了口罩
聽不清楚是不是你在說話

來自不同地方的水果
各有各敘說自己的故事
櫥窗有最新的構圖
革命孩子和新款鞋子押韻

我在你的食肆裏
碰上多年未見的朋友
在漬物和泡飯之間
一杯茶喝了一生的時間

還有多餘的銀幣嗎
商場裏可以買回許多神祇
她緬懷前生的胭紅
他喜歡市廛的灰綠

給我唱一支歌吧
在深夜街頭的轉角
我們與昨天碰個滿懷
卻怎也想不起今天

2003

Wu Li Painting by the Bay

Arrived from the ancient, exhausted Dynasty,
Here at Fragrant Mountain you've come to inquire
      for a boat with no fated time of embarkation . . .
And so you remain on the tiny island,
      listening to the sea winds whisper
That a new boat has already journeyed forth
      on an ocean voyage still more vast.
Your friend must already have passed the Equator.

Along the roads you seek the sounds of your native dialect,
      or the signs of spring plowing you know from home,
But all you can find are women in embroidered dresses,
      on streets strewn with flowers!
So you pick up your brush, and your whole heart leaps beyond
      what lies before your eyes—
The harsh, concrete sounds of the marketplace—
      returns to the landscape of your spirit's joy:
Beside the "fly head" characters you've been practicing,
      now you write only "bird claw" letters of that distant land.

On this sleepless night, you seem to hear
      vessels setting out for sea;
Early next morning, all you see are fishing boats
      bringing back fresh fish for Lenten luncheons.
In front of the steps of the great São Paulo church,
      fresh fruits of red and yellow are on brilliant display,
Black men are dancing in the streets—these strange customs,
These newly-minted sights, gradually blend with
      your daily routine.

吳歷在灣畔作畫

來自古老疲倦的皇朝
向香山索問卻未有船期
你滯留小島上，聽海風說
新船已邁進更淼瀚的水程
你的友人該已越過赤道了

沿路尋覓鄉音與春耕的風俗
只找到舖花的街上錦衣的女子
你端起筆來，一心超越眼前
具體的市聲，回到神逸的山水
你的蠅頭外邊盡是異地的鳥爪

不眠的晚上似聽見有船出海
早上但見漁舟帶回午飯的鮮魚
大三巴教堂階前擺滿紅黃鮮果
黑人在街上跳舞，陌生的風俗
隨新的顏色逐漸進入你的家常

太平無事的下午，你偷閒
舒開畫幅，想要繪畫故國山水
陰陽向背的曲折，不想短留
竟變成長居！歸途風雨還多呢
你的山樹上沾染了新的光影

1999

On this peaceful, uneventful afternoon,
      stealing a moment's leisure
You unroll a scroll to paint, thinking of depicting there
      the landscapes of your homeland.
In the vicissitudes of Yin and Yang, moving forward, backward,
      never did you think of lingering at all,
Yet the visit has now become a lengthy residence.
      Windswept rains when you return—surely, even stronger!
The trees on your mountains have been pervaded
      by a new radiance.

1999
Translated by Jonathan Chaves

Secret Family Recipes

the swirling flicker begins from a lamp
an always unsustainable accident at your ear
some say you're hot-tempered but you're already
no longer that; people later on
boiled that dish dry, forgot
the original theme, as we stirred
we slowly lost ourselves
too vague, too weak, too compromised
impossible to arrive at the shape of dawn-to-dusk thought
from beyond a mediocre cuisine we keep on wanting
to recover those lost notes

no matter where we go we always carry with us
from our youth the aromas that drifted through
lanes and alleys from large colonial houses after school
from the faraway town, renewing our desires
the comforting embrace we repeatedly lose
grown up, the subtly sweet and bitter sourness
disclosed in unavoidable depression
the secret escape route whose direction is unknown
eternal secret, stuck between the teeth like
Granny's paradoxical fishcakes:
an undifferentiated blend of sweet and salty

if you have the best bacalhau, if you have
Portuguese olive oil, strong and mellow enough
can everything be magically reproduced?
the dinners our godmothers cooked for us on Sundays
in every attic, behind every closed curtain and
shutter inside southern European-style windows
in these dusty yesterdays, what was subtly shining?
sisters recorded it, kith and kin noted it down
and the paper slowly and gradually faded
impossible to hold on to these mysterious rites
performed with such wizardly perfection

家傳食譜祕方

從一盞燈旋轉的閃爍開始
永遠無法持續的意外在耳邊
有人說你是辛辣的但你已經
不是辛辣的，後來的人
把這道菜煮得太乾，忘記了
原來的主題，我們在攪拌中
逐漸失去了自己
太模糊、太軟弱、太妥協
難以達到朝思暮想的形狀
我們繼續在平庸的烹飪以外
想去尋回那些失落的筆記

不管去到哪裏我們總帶着
童年放學經過巷道間
那些殖民地大屋中傳出的香味
來自遙遠的市鎮，修葺我們的慾望
是我們屢屢失落的安慰的懷抱
成長時那微甜的苦酸
在那些無法逃避的沉悶中
發現了逃走的暗道卻不知通往何方
永恆的祕密，如牙縫中弔詭的
老祖母的魚餅：無法分辨的
鹹和甜的混合

要得有上好的百加休魚，要得
有夠強夠醇的葡萄牙橄欖油
然後那一切就可以像魔法般重現？
教母在星期天晚上給我們煮的晚餐
在某一個閣樓，某一道闖上的
南歐風味的木窗裏面窗帘和窗罩下

remember the flavours of aniseed and nutmeg
those balichão stir fries really mouth watering
remember Granny used to cook a mysterious dish
(neighbours all knew in the kitchen she'd do her stuff)
the aroma lingered, but after she was gone
there was no one who could blend the same flavours again
our nickname was muchi-muchi, and after school
whoever lost a bet invited the others to eat cha-cha sweet bean soup
we grew up between meals, faintly remembering
grown-ups had shown us a mysterious album
we just mix food in the pan, not knowing if we can reclaim those riches

2003
Translated by Brian Holton

那塵封的昨天裏，微微閃光的是什麼？
姊妹們曾經記下、親友反覆鈔寫
而紙張逐漸褪色了
難留下那無法挽回的
巫師般準確搬演的神祕儀式

記得那些茴香與肉豆蔻粉的味道
那些葡式蝦醬炒菜特別惹味
記得祖母煮過的一道神祕的菜
(左鄰右里的人都知道，是她下廚一顯身手了)
那氣味歷久不散，但自從她去後
沒人能再調出同樣的味道
我們被喚甜角的渾名，放學後
打賭輸了請吃雜豆渣渣甜湯
我們在零食間長大，隱約記得
大人們曾向我們顯示一本神祕的冊頁
我們攪拌鍋中食物，不知能否尋回那豐富

2003

Sheltering from the Rain in the Café Caravela

the rain began during our chat
unavoidable as our chat
the Portuguese in the shop were drinking wine
behind them, the boat that had sailed every ocean
had it really been a treasure ship?
now it has congealed into a shop sign

sitting by the shop we idly watched
the day-long rain pouring down and pouring down
and unavoidably tired by the dark green
reflection from the puddle of the small harbour
upturned chairs and tables waited for closing time, dogs
all gone too, café feasts drawn near to their codas

they'd all gone to *Xinkoudian*'s grocers
maybe talking politics, kowtowing to a new Goddess of Mercy
we few nostalgic incorrigibles
lingered on by the old shop
you said not long before there had been a gun battle
it all seemed ideal, but even here had not escaped

even you who took the long road from the tropics had buried your grudges
your kindness always feeling there was no way to change an ice-cold world
you wanted to go, but the Portuguese photographer said to stay
unavoidable that my friends wanted to go too
so many boats crossing the world's oceans
hoping everyone could find their own rain and snow or sunshine

unavoidable that so many tall block-printed buildings were going up
the sorry little alley watching each closed shop
we knew too that shabby little alley hadn't developed
into a peaceful place, but we could remember
we had gathered here to take a drink
trying to help each other relieve life's sorrows

1999   Translated by Brian Holton

在金船餅屋避雨

雨在我們的談話中開始
像我們的談話一樣無可避免
店內的葡萄牙人在喝酒
背後是遠渡重洋而來的
那真曾是一艘金黃的船？
現在凝止成為一塊招牌

坐在店前我們懶洋洋看着
滿天的雨水瀉下來瀉下來
而我們無可避免被困在
小巷水潭慘綠的反光裏
桌椅覆轉等待打烊吧狗兒也
散了吧小館盛宴接近尾聲了

他們都去了新口店的食店
也許談公事也許拜新的觀音
我們這幾個無可救藥的
懷舊的人留連在老店前
你說這兒不久前曾發生槍戰
一切未如理想這兒也不倖免

你從熱帶遠道而來的也曾埋怨
善心總覺沒法改變冰冷的世界
你要離去，葡籍攝影師倒說留下
無可避免我的朋友也要離去了
這麼多的船舶來往世界的海洋
希望大家找到自己的雨雪和太陽

無可避免更多刻板的高樓建起來
困處小巷看着各自關門的小舖
我們也知道陋巷未發展成一塊
安居的地方，但我們會記得
我們曾在此地聚首喝一杯酒
嘗試幫助彼此解開生活的憂愁

1999

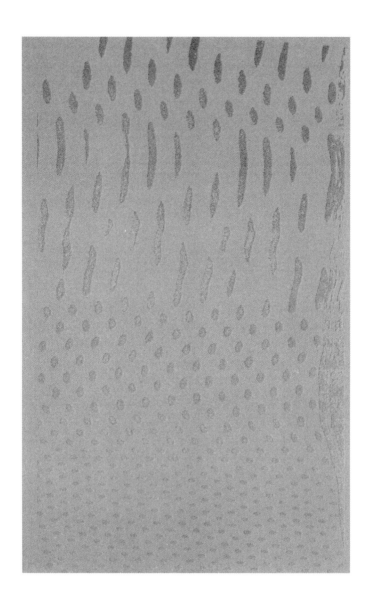

In Front of the A-Ma Temple

the temple is closed
even A-Ma gets time to rest
we'll just have to sit by the sea
and run our own maritime matters

drinking, we face the rolling grey waves
on the bottle gold characters celebrate Macau's return to China
today's weather is unsettled: cloudy or clear
when dusk comes it's a little stifling
the beer is cold enough
but can't slake our thirst

why are the distant hills split in half?
those plants drifting on the water
can they be leaves in self-banishment?
when, through layered clouds,
will break bright starlight?

1999
Translated by Brian Holton

媽祖廟前

廟關門了
媽祖也有休息的時候
我們只好面海而坐
治理自己的海事

面對起伏的灰色波濤飲酒
酒罐上有慶回歸的金字
今天天氣陰晴未定
黃昏來時有點翳熱
啤酒夠冰涼
可止不住我們的渴

遠山為什麼給劈開了一半？
那些隨水飄流的植物
可是自我放逐的花葉？
什底時候，雲層裏
會透出清明的星光？

1999

A Tapestry, Given by the King of Portugal
to the Emperor of China

1.

from the Paço da Ribeira
to the Yonghe Palace
from the mighty Don João V
was sent a messenger bearing other gifts
to be given to the Yongzheng Emperor

and a lofty diplomatic mission
to return a favour between the nations
to commemorate the Yongzheng Emperor's accession
to ease the severity of recent diplomatic policy
to guarantee the safety and the profits of the Portuguese in Macau

it boarded to the exalted sound of trumpets
crossed an endless roaring ocean
red silk backing crisscrossed with gold and silver threads
weaving out heroic deeds of officers of state
to be presented by one palace to another
each a residence protecting a Son of Heaven, from one mighty monarch
to another, on the admiring eye imprinting
heroic achievements, daily affirming eternal glory

2.

everyone knows
in nine pieces
packed in two wooden chests
the tapestry
was stuck in the bottom of the ship's hold
and first had to wait for the real-life wind direction
before it could set out on its voyage
then in Rio, in Brazil

葡萄牙皇帝送給中國皇帝的一幅掛毯

一、

從里貝拉宮
到雍和宮
由偉大的唐·若昂五世
派遣使者帶着其他禮品
一起送給偉大的雍正皇帝

背負了崇高的外交使命
為了兩國之間禮尚往來
為了慶賀雍正皇帝登基
為了緩和邇來的強硬外交政策
為了保障葡人在澳門的利益與安全

在高昂的號角聲中起航
越過波濤洶湧的無邊大海
紅色絲綢襯裏上面縱橫金銀絲線
織出了御前大臣的英雄事蹟
要從一所宮殿送往另一所宮殿
保護天子的居所，從一個偉大的帝皇
到另一個，在賞玩的目光中印證
英雄的業績，朝夕肯定永恆的光輝

二、

誰知道
分成九塊
裝在兩個木箱裏的
壁毯
獸在船艙的底層
先是等待現實的風向
才可以啟程
又在巴西里約熱內盧
等待雨季過去

waited till the rainy season was over
then sailed out for Batavia
stayed a month
waiting for provisions

meanwhile Don João V, King of Portugal
ate legs of lamb
drank wine
arrested commoners
erected magnificent buildings
celebrated his birthdays
dispatched armadas
went ashore on all sorts of islands
and gave orders for the weaving of tapestries
waiting for the recording of these things

and at this stage of waiting
the Yongzheng Emperor
also did things
he had people put to death
had people put in prison
carried out a Literary Inquisition
and the people he disliked
he had them dug up from their graves
to make them die again
he sent armies everywhere on punitive expeditions
and killed a good many people
while he was waiting
he did things like that
what was he waiting for?
No one knows
but maybe it included
the far-voyaging
narrative of immortal events
the heroic tapestry?

再航至巴塔利亞
停了一個月
等待補給

其間葡萄牙皇帝唐・若昂五世
吃了許多條羊腿
喝了許多葡萄酒
捕捉了許多平民
去建築許多宏偉的建築物
去慶祝他的許多個生辰
派遣許多艦隊
去登陸各種各樣的島嶼
又再下令編織許多壁毯
等待它們記載這許多事情

在等待的過程
雍正皇帝
也做了許多事情
他把一些人處決
把一些人關入大牢
推行文字獄
把他不喜歡的人
從墳墓裏挖出來
叫他們再死一次
他發動軍隊到處征伐
又殺死了不少人
他在等待的時候
就做了些這樣的事情
他在等待什麼？
誰也不知道
也許也包括了
遠道而來的

記述不朽盛事的
英雄的壁毯？

三、
英雄的壁毯
正在遠道向他航來
好像渡過了永恆？
不，只不過是
一年又兩個月的航程
什麼也沒有
除了日出日落
天氣的變化
除了生活
在潮濕和空虛中的
蠹蟲
每天來咬喫
一口一口的
把英雄事蹟
當早餐
午餐
下午茶
宵夜
一點一滴的
欣賞了
沒有什麼
留給
皇帝
大老
爺

1998

3.
the heroic tapestry
as it was sailing toward him on its long voyage
was it as if it had crossed eternity?
no, it was merely that
a voyage of one year and two months
was nothing
except the sun rising and setting
the weather changing
except for life
and moths
in the wet and the emptiness
coming every day to eat
mouthful by mouthful
for breakfast
lunch
afternoon tea
at midnight
bit by bit
enjoying it
so there was nothing
left for
His Majesty
the
Emperor

1998
Translated by Brian Holton

The Poet Camilo Pessanha Sleeps Curled Up on a Macau Bed

this is your world
stinking red hangings, enclosing
the iron bed on the Persian rug, the coloured blankets
enwrapping you who sleep curled up in layer upon layer
of the exotic scents of joss sticks and opium
faithful pekinese crawling close to you
licking your beard
your knees below your chin
as though you were mumbling new words
only the parrot repeats what you have said
you have abandoned all the houses on the other shore
and come here far across the oceans
roamed the earth to find a bed
no matter what turbid river flows outside
or where in the world its confluence
bishops and viceroys constantly changing
your eternity is a rosary
tear upon tear wept by an unlucky mother
you said farewell to every treasure in your past home
navigating between these Chinese relics in the mirror
your destination never reached, the scroll's flowers unwithered too
you leaned on the weathered blue and white porcelain
the Bodhisattva wound with spider webs
escaped the original order and drifted here
forever at rest, a fossil life
the peeling mirror reflects a bed of old blankets
folded into desires, carrying curses

詩人庇山耶蜷睡在一張澳門的床上

這就是你的世界
腥紅帷幔低垂，圍繞
波斯地毯上鐵床彩毯縱橫
把蜷睡的你包捲在層層
線香與鴉片的異香之中
忠心的北京犬爬近你
用嘴擦你的頭髮
你的膝蓋抵着下巴
彷彿在喃喃說新詞
只有鸚鵡重複你說過的話
放棄了所有彼岸的房子
你遠渡重洋而來
走遍地球找到一張床
不管外面混濁河流
在世界何處交匯
主教或總督換個不停
你的永恆是一串玫瑰念珠
坎坷母親的一滴滴眼淚
你告別了過去故鄉所有珍藏
在鏡中這些中國文物間航行
永不抵達，畫軸中的花朵，也不凋零
你倚偎着破損的青花瓷器
蛛網纏繞的菩薩像
離開了原來秩序流浪到此
永遠在休憩，生命是化石
剝落的明鏡照一床舊被
褶成慾望，帶着咒語

to put someone forever into a deep sleep
in this warm, narrow, humid cave
your woman of the East lit your opium pipe
you slept in a womb, you are a pupa
sunk in sleep you saw the demon that overflies reality
oh sleep, sleep well
things in dreams are more real
in those dreams you own
the whole world

1998
Translated by Brian Holton

教人一直沉睡下去
潮濕溫暖狹窄的洞穴
你的東方女人為你燒一口鴉片
你睡成胚胎，你是蛾蛹
沉睡中飛過現世的魅魎
睡吧，好好地睡吧
夢中的事物更真實
你在夢中擁有
整個世界

1998

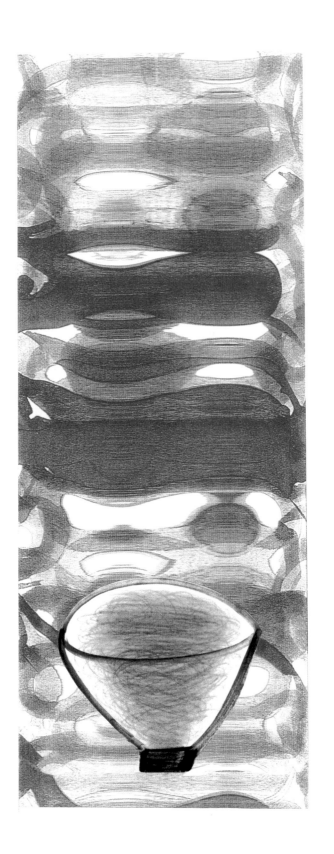

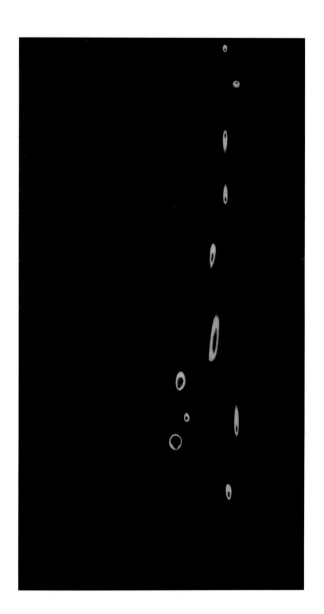

Brenesselsuppe

These scorching leaves
once scalded the hands that picked them
It's the poverty of wartime
cooked into today's ease
It's our family's homeless wandering
cooked into memories of home and comfort
It's the pine needles from our mountains
cooked into today's sweetness

It's pain bone deep
cooked into today's forgetting
It's bloated ideals
cooked into mustard for garnish
It's the grief of love lost
cooked into wan smiles
It's violent self-abandonment
cooked into fragile hopes

It's my bamboo village
it's your modest clothing
it's our parents' fears
it's our children's future
so fragmented
yet complete in the incompleteness
soothing years of sadness
quenching centuries of our thirst

wars are still raging
someone's sister is being killed
lives are in poverty
someone's true love is being lost
such unbearable marks remain
on the bricks of these ruins
can we grind them fine enough
to cook into a rich green soup?

1999   Translated by Helen Leung

蕁麻菜湯

是火燒一般的葉子
曾經灼傷採摘的手掌
是我們戰時的貧窮
煮成今日的從容
是親人的顛沛流離
煮成懷舊湯羹的家常
是我們山邊的針葉
煮成今日的甜美

是切膚的傷痛
煮成今日的遺忘
是巨大臃腫的理想
煮成粉飾的芥末
是失愛的苦惱
煮成淡漠的微笑
是狂暴的自棄
煮成瘦弱的希望

是我黃竹的鄉下
是你樸素的衣裳
是我們父母的憂患
是我們兒女的未來
細碎也真細碎
完整也未嘗不完整
解我們百年的愁
解我們千載的渴

仍有戰火在蔓延
仍有誰的姊妹被殺戮
仍有人活在貧窮中
仍有人失去她的至愛
頹垣廢壁的磚石
上面有難忍的印記
我們可把一切磨成粉末
煮成一窩鮮綠的濃湯？

1999

Poet in the Rome Airport

Who's the other traveller
sitting in the lounge with me
waiting for the transfer flight to the Slovenian Poetry Festival?
Another poet? Are there any recognizable marks?
Chubby or slim?
Man? Woman?
We'll be reciting poetry in a cave
acting as mysterious as spies
jotting down amidst the public clamor
traces of rain that soon will dry

Pretending to buy a croissant
just to feel the soft warmth of flour
the form and shape to be developed
the texture

He pretends to sit in a wheelchair
to feel the restraints of the body that cannot extend?
He's not agile, his thoughts are faster than his feet

He doesn't appear to be the one in dark glasses
wearing torn jeans and silver sandals
He may not be that fashionable
Donning a detective's trench coat?
Does he take in all the details
holding a pipe? but that's a bit too ordinary
He could be the bald guy in a humorous red T-shirt
Why not?

羅馬機場的詩人

那另外一位客人是誰？
坐在候機室裏，將要與我
同時轉機往斯洛文尼亞詩歌節
詩人，有明確的記認嗎？
肥胖，還是纖瘦？
是男？是女？
將要在山洞裏唸詩
行動詭祕如一個間諜
在眾人的喧嘩中默默記錄
轉眼就會曬乾的雨的痕跡

假裝買一個牛角包
其實是想體會麵粉的溫軟
可以發展的形體和線條
口感以及其他

他假裝坐在輪椅上
為了感受肢體不能舒展的限制
他笨拙，思想比腳走得快

他不一定是那個戴黑眼鏡
穿破牛仔褲和銀色涼鞋的
他不一定有那麼時髦
穿一件探長的長外衣？
他的確留意所有的細節
拿一個煙斗，那就未免太表面化了
他是禿了頭，穿一件可笑的紅T裇的那人
誰說不可能呢？

With a pair of keenly observant eyes?
Shy so as to protect something in his heart?
Reading a newspaper in sneakers he's had on since childhood
wearing a collarless black sweater
dark glasses, looking cool
or holding a bottle of juice, trying to look unassuming?
Half of him wants to ride with the wind, to drift away
the other half pulls him back to earth

That shorthaired guy in a yellow sports outfit
is attentively typing on his cell phone
sending text messages to God
This lady is wearing a particularly long dress
She must be hiding all her poetry
manuscripts in the pleats of her dress

Or is the poet the plump lady in the orange garment?
Squeezing two different persons into one body

2005
Translated by the Author

有一雙銳利的觀察的眼睛？

靦腆是為了老想保護住內心的一點什麼？

讀報，穿少年就開始穿的球鞋

穿一件無領的里毛衣

戴黑眼鏡，夠酷

還是拿一瓶橙汁，故意扮作平庸？

一半想逍遙飄逸乘風而去

另一半，把自己扯回地面

穿黃色運動衣的短髮男子

正聚精會神地用手機

給上帝發短訊

這位女子穿了一條特別長的長裙

一定是把所有詩稿

都收到裙底的褶縫裏了

又還是那個穿橙色連衫裙的胖女子？

她把兩個不同的人擠在同一個身軀裏

2005

The Beer House

There are so many types of beer
house brews
soothing
sweet
strange tastes
raw
and then there's the frothless
peaceful beer

Exhausted, we sit here talking
In a place where we cannot see
mysterious containers, coiling copper tubes
leading to countless cold vast oceans
each one originating from a particular region
crafted by a masked creator in a large black coat
each beer
with an individual character

Tired after walking so many roads
you ask if I'd found what I'd set out to seek
I've known the young and the mature
sometimes choked up
Those too sweet and bitter
bad tempered
possessive
admirers of Tarzan
or the Great Wall
They take a sip of me and shake their heads
thinking I'm not the beer their hearts desire

啤酒館

這啤酒館裏有各種啤酒
有店裏獨家製造的
平易順喉的
甜美的
味道奇怪的
尖酸的
也有不冒泡沫的
平靜的啤酒

走累了，我們坐在這裏說話
在我們看不見的地方
有些祕密的容器、盤捲的銅管
通往無數冰涼的浩瀚的海洋
每一種都來自一個特殊的產地
有個黑色大衣的神祕蒙面創造者
每一種啤酒
都有一種性格在背後

走過太多的路也就累了
你問我找到要找的嗎？
我嚐過年輕的和成熟的
有時也給嗆住了
總有太甜膩和太苦澀的
有脾氣的
佔有慾強的
崇拜泰山的
喜歡萬里長城的
它們喝我一口，然後搖搖頭
總覺得不是它們心中的啤酒

我們從城市的一端走到另一端
辦了太多事
遇到太多的人了
靜下來談談天
不是很好麼？
你是美麗又刺激的新酒
我是不冒泡沫的
平靜的啤酒

2001

We walk from one end of the city to the other
running too many errands
meeting too many people
slowing down every once in a while to chat
Isn't it nice?
You're the new wine, beautiful and exciting
I'm the frothless
peaceful beer

2001
Translated by the Author

The Poet and the Travel Guide

Waiting in the station for the train to Brugge—
a delayed train disrupts everyone's plans
people dash around in panic
only the poet is reading the travel guide seriously
which affirms the possibility of cultural exchange
For example, it states you will see the bell tower after climbing 300 steps
So, should we poets do precisely that?
No, I will not climb that many steps for poetry
that's not the kind of poetry I want to write
The city that became prosperous through trade and travel
had its destiny altered by politicians
the poet now wants to wake with a kiss
this ancient town that slept for 500 years, since the Middle Ages
The guidebook says there are small green slate lanes where carriages passed
overlooking the grand Gothic castle—and are there really swans
sailing elegantly on the lake? The poet has his doubts
He doesn't want to accept each numbered description
How can you be sure the restaurant at the square has the best lobster bisque?
He wants to open a mussel himself and taste it. Fresh green fields
gradually unfold before the eyes, dissolving into a moist patch
windmills and castles finally appear
pretty maidens and fresh fruit . . .
Taking back yesterday's sarcasm about Flemish Paintings
the poet is forever adjusting his vision

1994
Translated by the Author

詩人與旅遊指南

在火車站候車到布魯日去
遲來了一班車打亂了所有人的秩序
大家倉皇地追問去向
只有詩人在認真閱讀旅遊指南
旅遊指南老是樂觀地肯定文化交流的理想
比方它說爬上三百多級階梯就可欣賞鐘樓
你說我們寫詩的人就該這樣做？
不，我不會為了寫詩就去爬高高的梯階
我想寫的不是那樣的詩
因來往貿易而變得繁盛的城市
政客可以改變它的命運
從中世紀開始沉睡了五百年的古城
詩人卻在想要去怎樣把她吻醒
你說有馬車的得踏過青石板的小路
遙望哥德式巍峨的古堡，有天鵝在湖面
優雅地游弋？寫詩的人對此存疑
他不想全盤接受既定的描寫
未喝過怎能肯定廣場那片店有最好的龍蝦湯？
他要自己剝開青蠔咀嚼。青綠的田野
逐漸在眼前展開，緩緩地染成濡濕
終於出現了風車和古堡
豐滿的少女和鮮活的水果 ……
收回昨天對佛蘭德斯畫派的嘲諷
詩人是不斷調整視線的人

1994

A Chinese Delegation Tours Paris

A Chinese delegation is attending an important conference in Paris
To discuss the connection between today's world and the past
Representatives are here from each major Chinese province and city
Today is Sunday so they are touring around
Outside Notre Dame they take photos
On the tour bus the Chinese delegation sighs sadly
This famous place Paris never even had an impressive earthquake
As the bus passes Île de la Cité
Everyone can see where the Queen was imprisoned
Was it in Shandong or Shanxi where the most impressive earthquake struck?
Emperors everywhere had beheaded and been beheaded
We can say NO to Western Imperial Authority!
China also had emperors and revolutions
Countless heads were chopped off in Paris's Place de la Concorde
But when compared with China, whose revolutions led to more deaths?
That Napoleon guy has the biggest coffin
They supposedly found arsenic in his hair after he died
But imperial assassinations in China were certainly not inferior
We absolutely can say NO to western feudalism!
In Versailles gold and silver are everywhere
Glass mirrors are so shiny they make you dizzy
Seeing those gold inlaid pillars along the road
It is best not to let China's tomb raiders know about them
In the age of the Internet we worry
Foreign hegemony will infiltrate our local language
Our patented Chinese towns and villages
Are collapsing under their words
Driving through the tunnel someone asks
Is this where Princess Diana's accident happened?

中國代表團遊巴黎

中國代表團在巴黎開正經的會議
討論當前處境與過去的聯繫
有來自各省市的代表
今天是星期天出去參觀
在巴黎聖母院門外拍照
中國代表在車上慨嘆
巴黎這地方沒有一場像樣的地震
汽車經過河中的小島
大家看見皇后被囚禁的地方
是山東還是山西有過最像樣的地震？
到處的皇帝斫人頭與被人斫頭
我們可以對西方的皇權說不！
雖然中國也有皇帝和革命
協和廣場上還不是同樣丟了許多頭顱
跟中國比較誰的革命死得人多？
拿破崙這傢伙有最大的棺材
據說他死後頭髮發現了砒霜
我們中國皇室暗殺並不遜色
我們盡可以對西方的封建說不！
凡爾賽宮到處都是金銀
玻璃鏡子照得人昏了腦袋
路上看見那些鑲金的柱子
最好不要讓中國的盜墳者知道
在網絡時代我們擔心
他們的霸權抹煞我們的方言
我們專利的鄉村
正在他們的言語底下瓦解
駛過地下隧道入口就有人問：
可是戴安娜出事的地方？

Arriving at a famous bistro among flowering bushes

The Chinese delegates lounge in a salon for French celebrities

Concerned that the West's problems will be as difficult to digest as the food

Suffering a bout of diarrhea in Proust's home town

We can say NO to fresh salmon!

Isn't the omnipresence of commercial ads yet another form of hegemony?

Western toads hiding in the lilac garden

We are wordless in the shadows of leaders

Taxes are very high in France

Our politics even more unpredictable

Briefly glancing at France's historic sights

Buying up perfume as gifts for nine relatives back home

National customs are hard to transcend

Their people are quite fortunate

Special interests are even more unrestrained

But we can always say NO to anything!

We all have strange connections with our pasts

2000
Translated by Glen Steinman

來到花叢曾是有名的酒館
中國的代表坐在法國名人的沙龍
只怕西方的問題與食物同樣不易消化
在普魯斯特的故鄉拉肚子
我們可以對鮮三文魚說不！
老說商業世界不正是另一種檢查？
紫丁香花叢裏有西方的蟾蜍
領導人的陰影不能言語
法國的稅挺高的
我們的政治更加起伏
匆匆一瞥法國的名勝
買甚麼香水送九個親戚
國情如此沒有辦法
他們的市民挺幸福的
專業利益更加逍遙
我們總可以對某些事情說不！
大家與過去有各種奇怪的聯繫

2000

Mao Salad at the Paris China Club

You walk down the stairs
returning to a fabricated Shanghai
lights flickering
swaying the fin-de-siècle of our minds
in the crowded dark shadows
a past we have never taken part in

Why is the salad's last name Mao?
Celery and pineapple taste fine
but with carrots they misrepresent their genealogy
They're more similar to Ho Chi Minh's revolution
than staples for the Long March
and there's no cured pork from Hunan
Are you sure the other ingredients
have not fled carrying nothing but their minds?

One afternoon they wander into a foreign land
sipping tea in Luxembourg Garden
The weather brings influenza
and nobody makes them a pot of hot soup
They toss down some pills with water
dreaming of hot tea to soothe their throats
Those exiled vegetables are alienated from their native land
It's hard to take root in a foreign language

巴黎「中國俱樂部」吃毛沙拉

從樓梯上走下來
彷彿回到一個虛構的上海
燈火明滅不定
搖曳着我們腦中的世紀末
黑壓壓的人影裏
一個我們未嘗參與的過去

沙拉為什麼姓毛？
西芹和波蘿味道不錯
卻與紅蘿蔔一同認錯族譜
更像胡志明領導的革命
不似長征的口糧
也沒有湖南臘肉
你可肯定其他作料
不都是帶着腦袋逃亡了？

異鄉的下午它們跑出去
在盧森堡公園喝一杯茶
天氣令它感冒
沒有人給它煮一鍋熱湯
白開水送下藥丸
希望暖茶令喉嚨舒服
流浪的蔬菜與故土脫節
又難在異鄉的言語中生根

Why is steamed rice here so difficult to chew?
You said it might be mixed with glutinous rice
To hide in other identities?
Or indulge in the nostalgia of a bitter era?
An accumulation of unresolved emotions
gnawing between teeth
Maybe they have toughened up
to rebel against a peasant tradition

China is a *cheongsam* on a calendar
You and I could easily become decorations on a bicycle
There is a lover's eye on the matchbox
Haute couture and cigarette butts form clubs
Blood and sweat or spilled soy sauce
neither blood nor fervor is convincing now
Onions and garlic meet again after a long exile
speaking in whispers long into the night

So many crisscrossing paths beneath the moon
Nobody likes the barking dogs but let's walk a bit farther
Has life in a foreign land made you weak?
We are children wandering far from home
On a night without leaders
tempted by curious whispers to sell our favorite toys
lingering in the small paths beside the new opera house
do you believe you can find a new home?

2000, Paris, for Sonia and Gerard
Translated by the Author

白飯為什麼這麼難以咀嚼？
你說它們可能摻了糯米
為了冒充其他的身份？
又還是在憶苦思甜？
積累了咬不開的情緒
咀嚼我們在牙床之間
它們也許是硬起心腸
對一個農民傳統的變節

中國不過是月份牌上的旗袍
你我輕易變成自行車的擺設
火柴盒上有愛人的瞳孔
所有的虛榮和華服
與煙灰盅的煙蒂組織俱樂部
流血流淚或是傾倒醬油
激情與熱血已不令人信服
蔥蒜經歷流亡與豉椒重逢
耳邊盡是有說不盡的話

月夜裏滿目縱橫許多小巷
沒有人迷戀狗吠但且再走一段
異鄉的生活令你軟弱了？
我們是還未回家的孩子
沒有領導人的晚上
奇怪耳語引誘大家出賣心愛玩具
在新歌劇院旁邊的小巷徘徊
可相信自己會找到新的家鄉？

2000　給桑妮亞與樹克

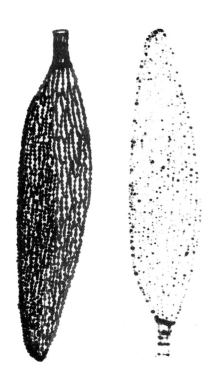

Love and Death in Vienna

We stroll along the broad corridors
looking at the respectable statues
with beards in different shapes

Sun and then rain comes
"The form people finally reach
can only be achieved through love."
Tell me, how does love affect
these variously shaped bearded faces?

In the classroom where corpses were dissected
we will recite poems about ghosts and specters
we will run a forum later, posing questions about
history, death and . . . how to be reborn?
Meanwhile, you keep talking about love for no obvious reason.

Walking past the fin-de-siècle corridors, our forms
constantly transform with light and shadow
Today you become spirited, not melancholic
I look at the reflection in the mirror of the cafe
The smile could grow heavy again, depending on
whoever arrives to coax out our kindness or cruelty

You walk around
a statue of a woman, contemplating
making out numerous forms
the statue of a muse
a snake
silently meandering beneath her feet

Must we dissect our chest in the classroom?
Disclose our hidden words in public?
Lines of poetry unconsciously seep out
taking shape after life's many injuries

維也納的愛與死

我們在寬敞的迴廊散步
看那些可敬的塑像
各自長着不同形狀的鬍子

有陽光，後來就下雨了
「人們最後達致的形相
唯有憑藉愛才可以完成」
你說愛情如何影響了
那些不同形狀的鬍子？

我們要在過去解剖屍體的
大課室朗誦鬼魂的詩
你待會要和我對談，問起
歷史、死亡和……如何再生？
現在你不知怎的老談着愛情

走過世紀末門廊，怎樣的愛情
令大家變成他們最后的樣子？
你今天變得輕快不再凝神？
我看咖啡室鏡子裏的反映
微笑可又變沉重了，端看誰
帶出了我們的殘酷和仁慈

一尊女子的雕像
你環繞觀看
看出許多不同的形狀
一尊繆司
一尾蛇
無聲在腳下蜿蜒

我們要在大眾的課室剖開胸膛？
公開說出心中隱藏的話？
不經意流露的詩行
經生活種種傷害成形

我們寫詩
我們愛與被愛
我們的容貌
經過陽光經過雨
經過愛
一點點地改變

一尾蛇無聲蜿蜒游過

2000　給老顧

We write poetry
love and are loved
our faces
through the sun, through the rain
through love
gradually change

A snake slithering past in silence

2000, for Kubin
Translated by the Author

Tasting New Sakes with Mio

a spring evening
cherry blossoms like flakes of snow
drifting close
staining the earth white
sidling over it
shadows

plain white vegetables
in red plum sauce
a freshly sour taste
steamed eggs, goose liver, in a shallow clay pot
a fullness
in simplicity

happy and sad perhaps
the encounters of people and events
leaving
and missing—our city
loving and worrying
dear ones who've fallen ill

a bit spicy
slightly sweet
milky white, unfermented
already a matured translucence
we tried one
then another

on the green-white vegetables
yellow sea-urchin eggs
a mild
freshly raw taste
cherry blossoms outside the window
blooming
falling
at the same time

2000, Tokyo. Translated by the Author

與羽仁未央試新酒

是春天的傍晚
櫻花像雪花
點點飄來
把大地染得緋白
上面有走過的
人影

素白的春菜
澆上紅色的梅汁
清新的酸澀
砵裏蒸蛋與鵝肝
樸素裏的
豐腴

有歡喜也有怨纏
經歷過的人事
離開了
又懷念的城市
摯愛又擔憂的
患病的親人

辛口的
微甜的
未經發酵的乳白
已經成熟的澄明
我們試了一種
又一種

青白的新菜上
醬黃的海膽卵
滿口素淡與腥鮮
窗外某處的櫻花
一面盛放
一面飄落

2000　東京

Thinking of John at Year's End

A cold wind rises from the edge of the sky
How's the sky on your side of the world?

I heard you were ravaged by floods
Gunter lost quite a few books
Living in the mountains has its challenges
water gushing out from the steep walls

I envy you now removed from these stacks of documents
No more endless meetings
No need to approve utterly meaningless proposals
to deal with bureaucratic documents and memos

There will be sun after the rain
Barbara will go on to care for 75 sheep
Rachael and Laura will meet new friends?
Your olive tree will bear fruit again?

You're closer to China after leaving China
Highlands and steep mountains open up to magnificent views
Perhaps you can be more attentive
and evoke ghosts from Liao's Study under lamplight?

You're under the sun in Southern France
I'm amidst smoke and dust on the island
When can we have another bottle of wine
sit around a table and go over lines of poetry?

February 2000
Translated by the Author

歲暮懷閔福德

涼風起自天末
你那邊的天空怎樣了？

聽說你們遭遇了水災
君特失去了好些書本
生活在山上有它的考驗
峻峭的山壁突然湧出洪水

羨慕你離開了千層文案
從此再沒有開不完的會議
不必審批毫無意義的計劃
應付官僚的鴻文和備忘

經過霪雨又會再是天晴
巴巴拉守着七十五頭羊
麗曹和羅拉交了新朋友？
你們的橄欖樹有收成了？

離開了中國更接近中國
拔地崇山通向奇詭的視野
也許從此你更可以專心
在燈下喚回聊齋的鬼魂？

你在南法陽光底下
我在島上處處煙塵
何時再來一瓶紅酒
圍桌細論詩的文字？

02/2000

Limes
—— for Gerard Morgenroth

You showed me the border ancient Romans left behind
On the way back, I asked you the meaning of the Latin word
You patiently looked it up in an enormous dictionary

We came to the border. Were there once
walls and fortresses? Beyond are infinite
possibilities and dangers. How often have I come to the end of a road
the borders of countries and territories, the borders of my knowledge
the borders of daily emotions, hesitating . . .

I hope you are still here, smiling gently
answering my countless questions
about all the drifting words in life

You always seem to have an enormous dictionary near at hand
You are the classic pillar, elegantly supporting the world
playing the clarinet, soothing, balancing our radical thoughts
hands on the steering wheel, steadily taking us
to where we wish to venture

How could I accept such sudden and tragic news?
Absurd accidents erase the human traces we value—
Are we no longer living in a rational realm?

You have shown us the skyline along the highway
Now the traffic on the crisscrossing roads has grabbed you
You who didn't mind crossing the border to support those in need
had indeed crossed the border we know
drifting farther and farther away

Like a swan sinking in the chill of water, people wake on the other side of time
I hope you find another farm, beyond this border,
where you can play your music even more serenely

10 Sept 2006
Translated by the Author

邊界
——給 Gerard Morgenroth

你指給我看昔日羅馬人留下來的邊界
倦遊歸來，問你這字的意思
你耐心地為我們翻開大字典

來到了土地的邊界，那裏昔日有
圍牆和碉堡？外面是無窮的可能和
危險？多少次我來到路的盡頭
國家疆土的邊界，個人知識的邊界
日常感情起伏的邊界，舉步猶豫⋯⋯

但願你還在這兒，溫和地微笑
回答我無盡的問題
關於人生中各種飄浮的字辭

你手上好似總翻開大本的字典
你是古典的廊柱，優雅地支持這個世界
吹奏單簧管，撫慰並平衡我們的偏激
手擱在駕駛盤上，穩當地把我們帶到
要去的地方去日

我如何可以接受這突然而來的噩耗呢？
荒謬的意外把一切抹去
我們不再活在理性邏輯的範圍裏面了嗎？

曾經指給我看路旁城市的風景綫
如今縱橫公路上的交通竟也傷害了你們
你這不介意越過邊界支持其他民族的
如今真的越過我們所知的邊界
愈去愈遠了

彷如天鵝沉進水的新涼，人醒在時間的那頭
願你在邊界的那邊，找到另一所音樂農莊
更優悠地玩你的音樂

10/09/2006

Notes on Translation

We have discussed it time and again, if there's a sentence
that can convey the feeling of things growing sparse, scattered

We seek peace in our hearts, in serene environs
exploring the limits of life's difficult times

Finding realistic details in abstract lines?
Seeing empty spaces in concrete descriptions?

Your detailed questions make me reflect
Can my words withstand such scrutiny, like fingers on a pulse?

In silence I send you my regards from afar
hoping you're recuperating from the operations

We both have had our adversities, refusing
to relate physical and emotional change in superficial language

attempting to feel, in places that avoid explanation
the unspoken words of each other

giving up the accumulated parts, changing
oneself, beginning again from zero

A new life, thoughts conceived in silence
from another, begun in solitude and taking new form

the unfinished words retained, leading to what follows
Not only the finished line, but the process of thinking

Thank you for wandering these meandering paths with me
walking together through these meandering lines in silent negotiation

2000, for Martha with best wishes for her recovery
Translated by the Author

有關翻譯的通信

我們曾來回討論有沒有一個句子
可以帶出那種逐漸疏落的感覺？

在環境的安靜裏找心的安寧
在艱困的日子摸索生活的底線

在虛渺的句子中找到現實的細節？
在實在的描寫中看見一點空白？

你的細問令我檢視自己
用的字眼經得起按脈的指頭？

我在靜默中想問候遠處的你
經重重的手術正逐漸康復吧

各自經過了悠長的逆境，拒絕
輕易的字眼敘說身心的感變

在沒有解釋的地方，嘗試體會
另一個人沒有說出來的那句話

獨自放棄累積的部份，更換
自己，面對零再重新開始

一個新的生命，永遠連接着另一個
孤獨的人，原來在沉默中想的話

保留前面未說完的，引向後來
不是結果，還有推論的過程

謝謝你與我一同走過這些彎彎曲曲的路
無言的彼此商量走出彎彎曲曲的句子

2000年初　給MC，祝健康

On a Friend's Book of Food

I carry your manuscript across Charles Bridge
thinking of what to have for dinner. There are blue crabs
With glutinous rice, sausage, mushroom and dried shrimp
perhaps I can throw together a pot of red crab rice

There are clams, but no friends
bringing wine over
the carnival of taste
requires an imagination broader than a recipe

Spicy food brings out sweat
porridge brings out woe
After swallowing down bitter bites and sarcasm,
one simply cannot abide the popular food trends,
expensive shark's fin and sun-dried scallops

One always meets the best vegetables late in life
We will hear frogs and mist from the sizzling fire
searching for a taste intimate and long departed
awaking the sleeping senses

Imagine a sadly magnificent eatery?
Imagine the most amorous process of eating?
Perhaps in the end we're simply looking for
someone who understands
not to overcook the chives

You stir up new weather and a landscape with chopsticks
you call upon misty clouds in hot soup
When can we share a good bottle of wine again
discuss young eggplants and old cucumbers?

Let's avoid mediocre hands and cook a table of new dishes
Savor the culinary arts of prose and brew good poetry
I'll be glad to help cut up green onions and garlic
to bring out the genuine tastes of your cooking

June 2006, for Yip Fai. Translated by the Author

為朋友的食經寫序

帶着你的文稿經過查爾斯橋
想今天該買甚麼菜，看見了花蟹
就不知有沒有糯米和臘腸、冬菇和蝦米
若有，也許可以湊合做一道紅蟳米糕？

有蛤蜊
欠的是攜酒而來的友人
味覺的狂歡
往往需要比食譜更大的想像

吃辣吃出了滿頭大汗
吃粥吃出了滿腹滄桑
吃過苦頭吃過冷嘲再難附和流行的食事
也不想盡吃鮑翅瑤柱的高雅

難得與明麗的新鮮瓜菜相逢恨晚
想在爐火咕嚕裏聽見蛙鳴和霧濕
想有一種久違又親切的味道
喚醒了沉睡的感官

想像一個最悲壯的進食所在？
想像一場最纏綿的進食過程？
也許到頭來不過是尋找一個懂得的人
不會把春韭做老

用筷子撥動晴雨山水
從熱湯裏可以看見雲霞
甚麼時候再共賞一樽好酒
細論嫩芯的茄子老去的黃瓜？

避開庸自煮滿桌的新味
細嚼散文的廚藝與詩的火候
讓我從旁幫忙細切蔥蒜
帶出你調理的真味？

2006　給葉輝